The Night We Landed on the Moon

The Night We Landed on the Moon

Essays between Exile & Belonging

By Debra Marquart

NDSU NORTH DAKOTA STATE
UNIVERSITY PRESS

Fargo, North Dakota

NDSU NORTH DAKOTA STATE
UNIVERSITY PRESS

Dept. 2360, P.O. Box 6050, Fargo, ND 58108-6050
www.ndsupress.org

The Night We Landed on the Moon: Essays between Exile & Belonging
By Debra Marquart

Library of Congress Control Number: 2021940038
ISBN: 978-1-946163-36-3

Artwork image provided by Licensor: "Suspension of Disbelief" © Duy Huynh
Cover design by Jamie Trosen
Interior design by Deb Tanner

The publication of *The Night We Landed on the Moon: Essays between Exile &
Belonging* is made possible by the generous support of the Muriel and Joseph
Richardson Fund and donors to the NDSU Press Fund, the NDSU Press Endowed
Fund, and other contributors to NDSU Press.

This is a work of creative nonfiction. The events are portrayed to the best of
the author's memory. While all stories in this book are true, some names and
identifying details have been changed to protect the privacy of those involved.

David Bertolini, Director
Suzzanne Kelley, Publisher
Kalley Miller and Grace Boysen, Editorial Interns
Zachary Vietz and Oliver West Sime, Graduate Assistants in Publishing

Printed in the United States of America

Publisher's Cataloging-In-Publication Data available from Library of Congress.

∞ This paper meets the requirements of ANSI/NISO Z39.48-1992
(Permanence of Paper).

For my mother, Gladys Marquart

&

in memory of my dearest friend and fellow poet, Barbara Crow

I had come from wondrous lands, from landscapes more enchanting than life, but only to myself did I ever mention these lands, and I said nothing about the landscapes which I saw in dreams. My feet stepped like theirs over the floorboards and the flagstones, but my heart was far away, even if it beat close by, false master of an estranged and exiled body.

—Fernando Pessoa, *The Book of Disquiet*

Contents

I.

And at the age of five ran away from home.
(I have never been back. Never left.) I was going perhaps
Toward the woods, toward a sound of water—called by what bird?
Leaving the ark tight farm in its blue and mortgaged weather.

—Thomas McGrath, *Letter to an Imaginary Friend*

Thirteen Ways of Looking at the Weather

The blackbird whirled in the autumn winds.
It was a small part of the pantomime.

—Wallace Stevens

1.

Footage of a tornado this spring morning on The Weather Channel. Tuberous as a taproot, it dips, retracts, stretches thin, then holds, taut as a sprung coil. Dark topsoil rises in spinning wisps as the funnel touches ground, widens, then moves like a vacuum across unfortunate Kansas.

On the flat horizon, the nub of a white clapboard farmhouse—a neat crop of outbuildings, a small stand of trees—disappears under the swath of wind, the funnel getting darker, spewing broken boards, strips of paper, sheetrock, metal. The caption on the bottom of the TV screen reads like a poem:

> *Danger*
> *Remains*
> *On the Plains*

2.

We didn't run to the basement like the weathermen say you should. No bracing in bathtubs or solid doorways for us. This was North Dakota, 1975—the time before Doppler, too deep in the country to hear sirens. Instead, we ran outside, into the swirl of wind, as country people do, to get a closer look at the weather.

In the wind-spun circle of our yard, between the house, the garage, and the barn—the well-worn path and turnaround spot where no grass grew—we stood and shielded our eyes as the dark sky moved above us. Our hair rose and fell in the currents. Our clothes lifted and whipped around our bodies.

Then in one split second, the wind fell to nothing.

The air hung around us, humid and time stopped. We waited in eerie, suspended quiet. And I remember Father pointing his bony finger straight up, directing our attention to where the sky had shifted to a violet gray.

We were in the calm center of something developing.

Overhead we could make out two strata of shifting clouds. One layer, low and dark, moved in a clockwise direction; and the other layer, light and touched on the edges by the sun, spun high and counterclockwise.

It was a true miracle of nature's coordination, I remember thinking. It was like that playground trick I could never master— spinning my right hand on my belly in one direction, and my left hand on the top of my head in another direction, all the while standing on one foot and whistling a familiar tune.

3.

When I tell my fiction class I'm writing an essay about midwestern weather, they break into spontaneous chatter. They are so brimming full of meteorological curiosities, anecdotes, and spare knowledge about weather, I cannot start class.

They turn to each other to gesticulate and gab, then they begin to shout weather stories at me, two and three at a time—the great flood and where they were, the big blizzard and who got stuck, the time they sat on top of a roof and watched bathtubs float by, the time they hunkered in the basement under a mattress and heard the tornado roar like a locomotive overhead.

Wait, wait, wait, I say. I can't include all these stories. I'm from North Dakota, the land of weather extremes. I have a head full of my own weather stories. I have to tell about the big blizzards of my own youth! The winter of '66—the way the snowfall fell so deep, it covered up whole houses. People chipped archway tunnels out of the snow drifts in order to get out of their front doors.

I have to tell about the time a few years ago in Fargo when four people died of exposure stranded in a car on 19th Avenue, only two blocks away from the NDSU campus. The passengers stayed with the car through the night and into the next day as you're always told to do: *Never leave the safety of your car.*

The streets were so socked in with snow, the drifts so high, they must not have realized they were still in the middle of the city. The workers found the car full of frozen people when they began to clear the streets. People talked about it for weeks. What a shame. If only they'd gotten out and walked, they would have been to someone's house in minutes.

4.

I have to tell about that spring afternoon in northern Iowa, 1995, on the way home from Minneapolis, when I drove unsuspectingly into high winds and threatening clouds, and how I parked on the side of I-35 in my Eagle Summit, listening to the National Weather Service interrupt NPR with that *EH, EH, EH* sound, then the electronic voice coming on (as if all living, breathing people had been destroyed and only this machine was left to warn us).

And the voice was saying, in patched together snippets of pre-recorded phonemes, that the National Weather Service has issued a tornado warning for Franklin, Butler, and Cerro Gordo Counties, and I remember thinking that I, personally, would have preferred a few names of cities, since I didn't yet know the counties in Iowa, and neither, I suspected, did the dozens of cars and semis lined up and down the road around me with license plates from Michigan, Oregon, New York, Pennsylvania, California and other far-flung (and soon-to-be farther-flung) places.

I knew for certain you must never park under the overpasses, as it is your instinct to do, thinking they are shelters, when really, they are wind-blown death traps that the tornadoes like to suck themselves under and smash things into.

And I remember wondering as my little car rocked side to side on its wheels, if I would know the exact moment when it was time to abandon the car, to throw myself into the ditch, face down in the grass, and dig my fingers into the clods of dirt.

Would I feel my car begin to lift? I imagined my burgundy wagon rising and spinning intact in the clouds, just as Dorothy's house had done in *The Wizard of Oz*, then being set down unharmed in some strange faraway land.

And in those long minutes on the side of I-35, as the rain blurred the windshield beyond seeing, I calculated that the car would roll to the east—the wind blowing in a northeasterly direction as tornadoes typically do—and so I moved into the passenger seat to avoid having the car roll over me when I bailed out, and I waited like that with my hand on the door latch.

5.

Confession: I never look out the window to check the weather. If I want to know what the day will be like, I turn on *The Weather Channel*.

Confession: I have one of those cell phones with Doppler radar and a satellite view of the weather. I often check it to see what's happening around me, weatherwise, even when nothing much is happening, weatherwise.

Confession: I like to watch *Storm Stories*. I'm fascinated by inclement weather and surprise storms. I enjoy anomalous weather patterns, as long as they don't involve me.

6.

In stories by Ernest Hemingway, the weather exerts a climate control over the plot, often pacing and foreshadowing calamitous events or unspoken secrets lurking inside the characters. When it finally hails or snows, or rains or blows, everything comes out—people crash and burn, they lose limbs, tempers flare, husbands confess infidelities, character flaws are finally revealed. Everything that was contained in the climate of the story from the first sentence comes out, but only the weather knows how the story will unfold.

7.

Sometimes I think the weather is trying to tell me something, but I'm missing the necessary equipment to decode the message, like when you accidentally dial a fax number and all you hear is that jangled buzzing on the other end of the line. To you, it sounds like noise, but you know it makes all kinds of sense to another fax machine.

I want to know what the lightning was trying to tell me that humid July night in southern Minnesota, 1980, driving home from the Kandiyohi County Fair gig with my band—the second-to-last of four one-nighters in a row spread across three states.

The road crew stayed behind with the bus to pack the equipment. The rest of the band climbed into the van for the long drive home. Usually, our bass player drove, or our keyboard player. After that, the guitar players would pitch in and take the wheel. But this night everyone in the band was too tired to drive, so I took over at two a.m.

I remember feeling responsible for lives that night as I drove. I could see them in the rear view mirror, all those trusting bodies sleeping in sprawls in the back of the van—heads resting on crumpled-up jean jackets, long legs thrown over armrests—and me in the front with only the sibilance of the radio and the column of headlights spreading before me on the dark road.

What causes me to remember that night so vividly, even now, is not what happened the next morning—the phone that rang too early. It would be the first in a succession of early-morning or late-night phone calls, strung out over the next few months, all of which began with the words, "I've got some bad news," then continuing with details of bus rollovers, drug busts, truck fires, lost equipment, embezzling agents, lawsuits.

But what causes me to remember that night so vividly is the storm that threatened, the lightning that came in constant flashes, illuminating the entire circle of the sky, one fragment at a time. And the variation! Soft puffs of heat lightning all around and large flashes that popped off. Explosions on the horizon, the tentacles of lightning that spread like arcing wires across the length of the sky, and the deadly bolts that cracked open the darkness high above and spiked a line straight to the ground somewhere in the unforeseeable distance.

For that night as I drove, the storm moved all around—before me, behind me, flashing on every horizon—but it remained elsewhere. It stayed where I was not. And no matter how long or how hard I drove toward it, I could not reach it.

It was the last unbroken night of my life.

8.

Weather stories, by nature, are subjective, full of nebulous and atmospheric detail, which is hard to capture in words—the piercing cold, your wet shoes, the pelting rain, the gales that shook the windows, the slush under the tires, that free glide of wheels on black ice when your steering wheel becomes useless.

Sometimes weather stories get long in the telling. They're like that made-for-TV docu-drama that your coworker wants to summarize for you during the coffee break the next morning, or the strange dream your lover or mother or sister suddenly remembers and wants to recount over breakfast.

You know the story will include confusing shifts in time, scene, and action, and that you'll have to listen along carefully and ask questions in the right places. You know you'll never really get the feeling.

You know it will probably end with "to make a long story short" or "I guess you had to be there." You almost hate for them to start.

9.

Weather theory: No conversation feels complete in the Midwest unless it includes some discussion, however cursory, of the weather.

Weather case-in-point: The movie *Fargo* begins with a long image of a lonely Minnesota highway that quickly dissolves into a white, snow-filled landscape. The movie is set in winter, which is unusual. Maybe snow is too hard to capture, or too expensive to recreate, or too uncomfortable to film in. Maybe film crews and actors don't like to stand around in the cold. For whatever reason, fewer and fewer American films feature winter landscapes.

So, the image of a snow-covered field is unusual to see in a film, but it is not unusual to see in the Midwest where snow is ubiquitous. In *Fargo*, a car finally appears on the road, emerging through the snowfall like a mirage. As it gets closer, we see that the car is towing a trailer with another car mounted on it. And so, the story begins.

The action of the movie turns on high crimes driven by the worst of human nature—kidnapping, embezzlement, grisly murders, one famously featuring a woodchipper. Police investigations ensue.

In one scene, Officer Olson, a small-town deputy, follows up a lead called in by a local citizen, Mr. Mohra. When Officer Olson arrives, Mr. Mohra is clearing his driveway.

Mr. Mohra leans on his shovel and gets to the point, passing along the information he has overheard—a funny lookin' guy out at Ecklund and Swedlin's, where he tends bar, was asking about where he can find a prostitute and bragging about how the last guy who said he was a jerk turned up dead.

"I understand." Officer Olson nods his head. "It's probably nothing," he says, when in fact it will prove to be their biggest lead. He turns to go.

"Looks like she's gonna turn cold tonight," Olson shouts back as he walks toward his car.

"Oh, yah, got a front coming in," Mohra answers.

"Yah, you got that right."

Fargo Weather Postscript: A fun thing to do in Fargo—the real Fargo, not the movie—is to drive around town with a four-wheel drive during snowstorms and rescue people. It's an austere landscape; you have to make your own fun.

On the coldest, snowiest nights, I've gone out in warm boots and good mittens with friends and found dozens of people to push and shovel out of snowbanks. In the middle of a rescue, if you discover that a driver doesn't know how to use his transmission to rock his car out of a snow rut, you feel embarrassed for him, like he's missing some basic skill for survival. You assume he's not from around here.

10.

The meteorologist for the NPR station in the university town where I teach is obsessed with the weather phenomenon, El Niño. To a lesser degree, he's also unnaturally interested in La Niña, El Niño's little sister. He's like the guy who keeps bringing the conversation around to the subject of his Corvette, or who only wants to talk about the stock market or the New England Patriots. Only, for him, it's All-El-Niño-All-the-Time.

He can segue to the subject of El Niño from any topic under discussion—corn futures, hog reports, poetry readings, shipping logs for Lake Superior, the pharmaceutical industry, the long-running success of the musical *Cats*. His weatherman voice is deep and comforting, like someone you'd like to hear reading you a bedtime story. And when he speaks of El Niño, there is something close to love in his voice.

But the months and years between El Niños must get long for him. I hear deep sighs after a forecast for another sunny day and whimsy in his warning about another thunderstorm. Garden-variety weather. He waits for the day when he can flex his El Niño muscles and explain again, in a way we can never hope to understand, the mysteries of the Southern Oscillation Index.

In the meantime, he contents himself with side notes and digressions, small tidbits inserted after a report on the New York fashion industry about the current meteorological indicators—how they point (or do not point) to El Niño's imminent return.

El Niño Postscript: In 1998, during an especially active El Niño season, a retired naval pilot from Nipomo, California, named Al Niño began to get irate phone calls from people accusing him of being responsible for the climactic changes. One man blamed him for the torrential rains and begged him to please stop them. A farmer accused him of causing his strawberry crop to fail. The BBC reports that another man called alleging that Al Niño had caused his daughter to lose her virginity, although it was never made clear what the weather might have had to do with that.

11.

My husband and I used to take long walks in the neighborhood after dinner. We said it was for the exercise. Really, it was just to get the bowels moving. We were eating too much and talking too little.

On these walks, we could chat about flowerbeds and trimmed lawns without fear of anything important coming up. We often passed by other couples from the neighborhood out for their nightly walk. Perhaps they too had stagnant intestines and stuck tongues. We'd smile and say hello. Sometimes we'd stop and comment on the pleasantness of the weather.

One night, my husband and I ventured too far, and at our farthest point from home, the weather suddenly changed. The air grew heavy as syrup. The clouds went from white to black.

We turned for home, breathing hard, sweating as if climbing uphill. A mist started to fall, the wind picked up. We broke into a run. Then lightning began to flash all around us. There was no thunderclap to follow; it was all soft, diffused light. Still it scared us. We ran home like this, holding hands, heat lightning flashing around us every few seconds, as if we were being photographed by the paparazzi.

By the time we got home to our stoop the storm had broken fully. We ran up the front steps, laughing hard and drenched clean through.

12.

Every summer, after another tornado hit some farm in my hometown, my father would pile us into the Chevy, and we'd drive out to survey the damage. On the way up and down the gravel road, we'd pass other families in their cars doing the same thing.

The tornado always seemed mysterious to us—judgmental, malevolent. Why had it taken the new house but left the old barn; why had it smashed the shiny Mustang to bits but left alone the rusted Ford; why it had leveled every last building, separated every board from every nail, but left unscathed the small shrine to the Virgin Mary in the front yard.

That afternoon in 1975, after our family stood in our yard and watched the funnel form above the farm, we grabbed each other and ran inside to escape the wind. Minutes later when the storm passed, we could see that the tornado had touched down one mile north of us on the Harrison farm. The buildings were mostly gone. Even then, the Harrisons were trapped inside the collapsed walls of their house with a young baby.

But when I think about this story, I realize that something is wrong with my memory of the day. Everyone in my family is present in the scene—my parents, my three older sisters, my brother—but, by 1975, we kids would have all moved away from home.

When I question my older sister, she reminds me that the tornado hit the day of Grandpa Geist's funeral. We had just come home from the cemetery, so that's why we were all at the farm together. And when she tells me this, I remember something I read years ago about ferocious storms, about how they sometimes coincide with the death of large-souled people; as if the atmosphere cannot handle this new element that has been loosed into its presence and must disperse it in torrents of wind and rain back into the world.

13.

In a 1924 brochure, created by the Northern Pacific Railroad and distributed widely in the eastern United States to lure farmers to new territories in the Midwest, the reader is encouraged to "Come to North Dakota!" The first page of the brochure features a line drawing of the North American continent. The caption above the drawing proclaims, "North Dakota: The Center of the North American Hemisphere."

In the drawing, lines coming from four directions of the continent all end in arrows pointing at North Dakota, which is shaded darker so that it appears to hover large above all the lesser states. The first line coming from the west coast reads, "not too dry." The second line coming from the east coast reads, "not too wet." The third line, coming from the Gulf Coast reads, "not too hot." And the fourth line originating in the Arctic Circle reads, "not too cold."

The text at the bottom of the page explains that "extremes of temperature to which the state is subject are not unpleasant due to low humidity. Hot, muggy days are very rare in summer and long twilight periods and nights are always cool. . . . The winters are cold, but it is the dry, crisp, clear cold that is more healthful and more pleasant for man and beast than the winter weather of regions of so-called moderate climates." The infamous dry heat and dry cold. Were there ever more useful weather euphemisms?

Lewis and Clark, in journal entries describing the Corps of Discovery's encampment in what is now North Dakota near the Mandan villages during the winter of 1804–1805, note the temperature regularly: January 7, 1805, −20°F; January 9, −21°F; January 10, −40°F

72° below the freesing point, Clark writes.

The journal entries are full of references to the cold, to frostbitten limbs, frozen toes. The Mitutanka, the village of Mandan closest to the Corp's encampment, appear often, checking on the expedition. Sometimes they answer Lewis and Clark's questions about what they know about the territories lying west. They visit the fort, accompany the expedition hunters to find food. One wonders how differently the history of western expansion might have unfolded if the Mandans had neglected to check on Lewis and Clark, if they had feigned ignorance when asked to provide a "Scetch of the Countrey as far as the high mountains."

But the Mandan people did not leave Lewis and Clark to freeze or flounder. Maybe they could not? For an unspoken code exists in cold landscapes—silent watchfulness for acts of stupidity by the uninitiated, followed by begrudging helpfulness once the forces of weather have outstripped arrogance.

And so we are here in cold places. And so I have my own stories of −20°F nights that I tried to drive through in North Dakota—whether through stupidity or desperation.

Like once, a little drunk in the 1980s, 2:00 a.m., after the amorous advances of my married boss during a company Christmas party, when I stormed off in my Plymouth Fury. I took the long, frozen artery of Main Street through Fargo to be safer, navigating by peering through the two-inch porthole I'd chipped out of my icy windshield.

All along Main Street as I drove, I could make out the shapes of abandoned cars—makes, far more expensive, and models, far newer than mine—all of them frosted-over, as if powdered with sugar, parked at odd angles just where they'd stalled or been pushed at odder angles onto the side of the road. It looked like Mars or the Moon to me then, some alien, inhospitable landscape.

Nothing you've heard about −20°F cold is an exaggeration. Any attempt at description is a reduction in terms, a failure of language. Spit does freeze before it hits the ground. So does piss. Any part in your car that's weak will break. Your pipes will freeze and burst. Those nights, I would set my alarm clock for every two hours, so that I could go outside and start my Plymouth Fury to warm it up. Otherwise, it would have been a solid block of un-startable ice by morning.

But the Fury never failed me; it never left me on the side of the road. Not even that that −20°F night, coming home from my husband's grandmother's funeral in South Dakota. Almost midnight, thirty miles from Fargo, our gas line began to freeze. We lurched and stalled on the side of I-94.

I got out and lifted the hood of the Plymouth to prime the carburetor, unscrewing the butterfly nut, lifting off the lid of the air cleaner, and propping the flap of the carburetor open with a ballpoint pen, then pouring the liquid Heet straight down into the engine's gullet.

My husband sat behind the wheel, grinding the ignition and gunning the gas, until the Fury roared to life. Then I'd hop in and we'd proceed another three or four miles down the freeway until the car choked and we'd have to repeat the process again. We made it home that way, those last thirty miles, in three-mile increments.

By now, I've forgotten the precise feeling of cold, and I can't recall why I was the one who got out and worked under the hood while my husband stayed warm behind the wheel. It was my car; I suppose I understood its workings, and I was always better with machines.

But how to capture in words the feeling of the air that night—crisp and rarefied; clear, still skies; unadulterated winter; capital-C cold, like the sound of one thin violin note stinging through the air.

I'm certain we were worried as we struggled with the Fury, and I suppose we were on the brink of extinction. But what I remember most is that we were not alone out there. Each time I got out of the car, I heard the sounds of other people stranded along the road—hoods and car doors slamming in the distance; people talking and calling to each other in the cold night; and laughter, I swear, somewhere out there it sounded like a party was going on.

Each time I jumped back in the car and we lurched forward, I didn't even try to tell my husband what I'd heard out there. Some things about weather are too hard to explain, and some things are even harder to believe. Sometimes when weather gets that bad, all that's left for you to do is put your head down and laugh right into the teeth of it.

Losing the Meadow

Neither my father nor my mother knew
the names of trees
where I was born

What is that
I asked and my father and mother did not
hear they did not look where I pointed
                    —W.S. Merwin, "Native Trees"

Iowa, a cool spring morning with the windows open. The robins are saying *cheer up, cheer up*. Mourning doves coo, and crows swoop down, cawing as they pick through a bag of garbage that one of them has dragged from the dumpster and spread across the driveway.

The lawn outside these windows is edged by a row of untended trees and shrubs that provide cover for all these creatures, including the rabbits who creep out in twos and threes in the morning and scuttle back under the tangle of vines at night when my headlights swing around back to park in the underground garage.

Until recently, on the other side of this grove, a creek trick-
led through steep wooded banks, and beyond that was a large
pasture with rolling slopes and an unpainted barn. As many as
six horses swished their tails in that meadow during the day as I
worked. Sometimes when I got stuck, I would put down my book
and watch the horses grazing, watch their long necks bend to the
grass, the muscle of their withers flexing to the rhythm of chewing. Sometimes on snowy days, they would cluster on the wind-
break side of the pole barn and nuzzle each other, their manes
riffling in the breeze.

This morning, if only for the company of the birds, I'm grateful for the presence of these few remaining trees—a mixture of
ash, maple, and oak trees with a leafy understory of wild plums
and mulberries that produce fruit that will fall to the ground and
rot by the end of summer.

Whoever landscaped this complex when it was built in the
sixties must have loved fruit and flowering trees. Along this short
street, Pinon Drive, are dwarf apples, crab apples, and redbuds.
They ring the recreation area at the end of the cul-de-sac in perfect intervals even as the small pool and tennis court grow more
paint-chipped and decrepit.

From my second-story windows, for the last nine years, I
have watched these trees in every season—greening, blooming,
and going to yellows and oranges in the fall. One winter morning after an ice storm that paralyzed all movement in the city
for three days, I emerged from the dark underground garage in
my car only to be blinded by bright prisms of sunlight reflecting
through the limbs of these trees like ice-glazed sculptures.

Farther in the distance, beyond where the horses grazed was
once a small pond, not a swimming hole, but enough to provide a
shimmering mirage like a slim coin of silver from the distance—
enough to give the frogs something to sing about at night. Closer, standing tall in the mid-distance, there remains a dead tree

whose stripped-smooth trunk and limbs jut into the sky in bone-white silhouette in both sunlight and moonlight.

The pasture that the horses grazed in was described as a meadow in the newspaper ad that I answered nine years ago—*apartment overlooking a meadow*. I was going through a divorce, and even though my husband and I agreed that none of it would be unpleasant (we'd never fought, and we would not start now), making the call affirmed some reality I hadn't yet faced. Perhaps it was only the encouragement of the word "meadow" that allowed my fingers to dial the number.

The receptionist at the management company transferred me to Ed. In Ames, Iowa, a small college town where trade in apartments is big business, most of the listings are held by a handful of companies, and Ed's was one of them. He said he had several apartments that fit that description, and he would drive me around to look at them later that morning. He suggested that I drop my car at the Kum & Go. (This is really the name that someone decided to give a convenience store chain in Iowa, and I see no reason to conceal it.)

I suppose I should have been cautious about leaving my car at a gas station and driving off with a complete stranger. It's the kind of red-flag detail that causes you to shake your head in disbelief after a woman's disappearance. I don't imagine that I was thinking clearly during that time, on the verge of ending a fourteen-year marriage. Besides, it is a small college town, and Ed was the owner of the company.

On the phone, he told me to look for a yellow Cadillac, which, my God, it was—not canary yellow, but closer to banana pudding. The car looked a mile long idling in front of the Kum & Go. Ed got out to shake my hand, looking pleasantly surprised as if he'd already sized me up as a suitable tenant—the girl who sought a meadow apartment.

He was tall, with a forward list in his walk—in his sixties with a full head of silver white hair and a deep golf tan. His shoes were white, and he wore a polo shirt that matched his car. We introduced ourselves and jumped into the caddy, heading south on South Dakota Avenue toward the edge of town where there were still rumored to be meadows.

It's only several blocks from the Kum & Go to Pinon Drive where the rental properties were located, but in that time Ed managed to get a lot out of me: that I didn't have children so I'd be living alone; that I'd wanted children but wasn't able to have them; that my husband was ten years younger than me; and that I was leaving the marriage, in part, because I wanted him to have a chance at having a family of his own.

Maybe it's the Midwest, maybe it's Iowa, but people manage to get the critical details pretty quickly. Having moved here in 1991 from North Dakota where people are no less curious, but more reticent about asking probing questions, I'd learned by then to just let the information flow out of me. I figure, Iowans are going to construct a story about where you're from and what you're doing here whether they get the true facts or not, so you might as well let them start with good information.

The questions seemed reasonable in the context of property management, trying to assess how many bedrooms and bathrooms I would need, how much square footage. I confessed to Ed that I'd originally imagined moving to a farmhouse somewhere in the country. I'd had a recurring dream about sitting on a porch in a rocking chair and watching the sun rise directly out of an open field, although I didn't tell Ed that.

I had already answered several ads for farmhouses that had been discouraging—tiny kitchens and closets, unfortunate linoleum choices, floor-to-ceiling fake wood paneling, and the troubling mustiness in the air that signals the occupation of mice.

One woman I called wouldn't even agree to show me the small guesthouse she'd advertised that sat on her property. She lived in the main house on the acreage and would only consider renting to a young man, she told me, who could shovel her walk and driveways in the winter. As a forty-something woman who'd just been declared officially barren, I was already feeling superfluous. I didn't even attempt to make the argument that I was a born-and-bred farm girl who could shovel as well as any man.

I learned from Ed that he owned much of this open land on the southwest side of town, which included patches of development, a rough-wood condo complex with a curved driveway, a brick hospice with a gazebo and a massive green lawn. These buildings were surrounded by postage-stamp fields of corn and soybeans that gave way to woods that descended into the small ravine of the creek and to the open fields spreading to the highway.

I'd always liked the rustic feel of this side of town, the way it blended to open country. The lone red barn on South Dakota Avenue that threw a tall shadow could easily be imagined as an artist's studio.

I don't know when or how Ed came into possession of this land, but it had been a smart move—the city had grown right into his hands.

As we navigated the intersection of South Dakota and Mortensen in the yellow caddy, Ed pointed to his right and said, "There's a farmhouse for you to rent."

The property on the corner that he pointed to seemed to be disassembling before our eyes—grass worn thin, overgrown bushes, and a half-standing fence with broken posts. In the back of the lot, abandoned vehicles rusted where they had died or had been pushed, and unpainted outbuildings tilted at angles.

I estimated that this was the original farmstead to which all of this land had once belonged, and I wondered about the woman who had planted those lilac bushes. How would she feel if she could see her yard in such disarray, with the city spreading around her front door? Ed told me that the property had just become available again. If I was interested, we could stop and look at the farmhouse after he'd shown me the apartments.

We turned left onto Pinon Drive, passing by look-alike bungalows with attached garages all in rows. Ed parked the car and showed me inside one, but the bedrooms seemed too small, the ceilings too low. That icky feeling came over me, the one I imagined I would feel each morning waking up alone in this place.

"Let's keep going," I said, remembering the promised meadow apartment. We got back in the car and drove to the cul-de-sac at the end of Pinon. These two large buildings, he explained as we parked, had been designed for older tenants downsizing from family homes. These are known as "professional" buildings in college towns. My neighbors would be retirees, college professors, medical interns, and carefully screened graduate students—all people who were unlikely to party until 4:00 a.m. on the rare occasion upon which Iowa State University won a football game.

We passed through the foyer, which featured a cathedral ceiling and transom windows above the doorway, a wraparound staircase that led to the second floor, and a chandelier hanging high in the center. It must have been a grand building when it was new. But now the handrails were loose, the carpet was fraying on the edge of each step, and the scuffed walls were painted a toothpaste mint green with a floral pastel wainscot.

Still, I could feel the solidity of the place, no trampoline effect on the floors when you walked. And the walls were thick, no stereo or TV sounds or the screaming of children leaking from behind doorways. I was thinking, *I'm really doing this*, when we reached the three-bedroom apartment at the end of the hallway.

The door unlocked to an open kitchen, a dining room and living room larger than any apartment I'd ever imagined trying to furnish before. I started to imagine it. Ed asked me if maybe this was too much space for one person. I told him that I had hoped to someday adopt a child—which I did—but I also knew that I had plenty of books that I'd never been able to put on shelves.

How does one block out plans for a new life? How much space is enough to imagine growing into, and when does having too much space risk feeling cavernous and lonely?

The master bedroom had large corner windows, allowing a view in two directions, like a hideaway perch overlooking the world. Ed showed me the walk-in closet, the mirrored vanity area, the second bathroom, all of which I admired for his benefit.

But what I remember most about the master bedroom was the way the sun streamed in the northeast window and that when I looked out the window for the first time, I saw the horses grazing in the rolling green pasture, and I had the immediate thought, *I could work in a place like this.*

Several minutes passed as I stood looking, trying to decide what to do. Signing a lease would be an irrevocable act. Maybe Ed left me alone for this time. I lose track of him here in my memory, and only become aware of him several moments later watching me from the doorway. And when I turn to notice him, I see myself for a second through his eyes—a fragile woman, sad, standing in the sunlight.

"How much is the rent for this apartment?" I asked. The figures had risen with each place he had shown me, and this was clearly the finale. Maybe I imagined it, but I thought I could see that he wanted me to have the place, perhaps for selfish reasons—I'd be a steady tenant—but I also believe that he could see how badly I needed a place like this.

He hesitated, then looked down at the beige carpet and said, well, normally this apartment would rent for around $900, but he could tell that I'd live lightly on the place, so I could have it for $700, if I promised not to tell anyone what I was paying.

Cool evening as I finish this, early fall. The trees serve as a gathering spot for the deafening insect symphony—the cicadas, the crickets, the grasshoppers—as well as the tree frogs and the occasional barking dog. I can pick out most of these sounds as they rise and fall, although I must admit that I'm not certain what sound grasshoppers make. And every so often I hear a slow ticking sound that rises through the mix made by a creature that I'm also not able to identify.

It's a complex layering, the acoustic evidence of things out there that I've always found comforting during the long mild autumns in Iowa. On these nights, I like to sleep with my windows open, listening to these pleasant sounds without being awoken by the window-rattling car stereos of someone coming home at 2:00 a.m., or the whining escalation of someone's motorcycle racing down South Dakota Avenue at 4:00 a.m., or the garbage truck with its back up beeper coming at 6:00 a.m.

This is the quintessence of early fall to me—the night sounds of insects, the wind in the trees, the semi-cool breeze coming in the window, the three-tone wail of the train moving through town. And what's that other sound in the distance? Ah yes, the ever-present hum of someone's air conditioning unit.

I will tell you something strange. When I moved to Iowa in 1991, I thought there were altogether too many trees. They blocked my view of the sky. I could never see the moon! That's when I realized I was irrevocably marked by North Dakota, a place of flat, unbroken horizons. In the Dakotas we only have naked clusters of trees in the middle of an agricultural field, the last vestiges of where a farmhouse once stood. We have woodland corridors along the occasional lakes and rivers, volunteer Russian Olives in the ditches, and mature groves surrounding farmhouses.

So this has made me a lifelong stranger to trees. As a North Dakotan, I've only known a few woodland species personally enough to speak of them with any certainty—the lilacs that marked the edge of my grandmother's backyard; the giant cotton-woods by the chicken coop on the edge of our farm that let out loose white puffs in the spring; and the chokecherries in the orchard bordering our family land that we picked fruit from in late summer for canning, the sweet grit of the cherries as we popped them in our mouths on the way home even with the light dust from the gravel road still on them.

During my time in Iowa, I have come to know a Kentucky coffee tree that sits outside my office window in Ross Hall. Even before I knew its name, I sensed that my tree must be something of a celebrity. I would look out my office window and see forestry professors with groups of students circling the tree, stroking its bark, pointing to its roots, examining the folds of its leaves as students jotted down things in notebooks.

I became so curious about my tree that I searched and found its name on a forestry department website that catalogs and identifies significant trees on the ISU campus. But I'm only able to retain the name because I've come to know it so intimately over the years through the frame of my third-floor window—spending ten- to twelve-hour days working in my office, always looking up from my desk to find it, taking comfort in the silhouette of its branches against the backdrop of the sky as it changes from soft blue to indigo.

Many afternoons, I've watched crows perch in the Kentucky coffee tree's branches in artful and ominous configurations, as they peer in on me, strange creature toiling away inside the lighted window, then caw and reel off into the sky to join the clusters of crows that gather in Hitchcockian numbers to blacken the treetops around our campus.

I come from generations of people who can tell you the names of birds, flowers, grasses, and trees, but I did not seem to inherit this talent. I try, I try. I study the particulars—needle-like or broadleaf, compound or simple leaf, types of bark and trunks—but the names still fall out of my head, even as I struggle to memorize them. In order to remember a tree, it seems, I must know it over a period of time, through seasons, in my eyes, hands, and blood.

Yet, even as an itinerant musician and artist who has spent her time out in the world as a renter and not an owner of property, it appears I have unconsciously followed my pastoral leanings. If I list the apartments that I've lived in since leaving the farm for college in 1974, I can see that I've always chosen high places with large windows overlooking green spaces. I've looked for mature trees in the distance, apartments that stand on the undeveloped edges of cities—the view that most closely resembles the prospect from my childhood bedroom on the farm.

And as a renter and not an owner, I have experienced again and again the helplessness of losing these green expanses. Maybe a year or two of this bliss, then the first troubling signs appear. Maybe the horses disappear one day, as mine did. Hard to know if they were really gone when I last checked, or just grazing on the far end of the pasture. Sometimes on walks you could approach them on the avenue side, and they would lean across the chain link fence, sniff the air with their dilated nostrils, and allow you to stroke the velvet of their broad smooth foreheads.

So maybe out of curiosity, I decide to venture into the meadow along the creek and that's when I notice the wire stakes with the orange flags on them, stuck into the ground by the gas and power companies to guide the excavators who are coming in to do the digging. Could the yellow earthmovers be far behind? Following that are the incessant sounds of backhoes and front loaders, and then the construction sounds—the backing up of dump trucks and later the hammering of the carpenters that starts so early and goes so late.

Then one day I look out the window and notice that I can't see the thin blue wafer of the pond in the far distance anymore, which causes me to wonder where the frogs had to go. And that night I notice, instead, the bright funnel of a streetlight shining down where the pond used to be. Then I check again the next morning and finally see the thin band of pavement that now runs through the space where the pond used to be, as well as the red realtor signs posted at neat intervals marking the lots available for purchase, and, yes, already there is a power walker wearing a pink headband making her way along the freshly plumbed-in street.

Soon, through the cover of leaves I will begin to identify the wood frames of large houses taking shape, and it finally occurs to me to climb the fence despite the "No Trespassing" sign that's been posted. And when I do, I see the meadow—or the pasture, or whatever we decided to call it—entirely gone, as is the creek. And I can't help but wonder what they could possibly have done with the creek. But it's gone down to a trickle, as are the dozens of trees that hugged and followed its contours, and now several backyards are being leveled out in fresh black dirt where the deep roots ran, where the flowing water and the sharp rocks and steep inclines of the creek used to be.

It's hard to know if all this began after Ed died in 2004, because I didn't learn about Ed's death until a year later, and I only realized it when his son, Ed Jr., sold my building to another management company, who sold it to another management company, all of whom introduced themselves in cheerful flyers left in the crack of my door announcing that they were thrilled to take possession of my lease and eager to please me, the corporate addresses of each successive owner coming from places farther and farther away from Ames, Iowa—Des Moines, Chicago, Newark.

Long before that, the older couples on the first floor began to die off or go to nursing homes never to be heard from again, and the math professor moved back to Italy, and the medical intern became a general practitioner and moved his small family to a house. And then it was just mostly me here in the building with a few nice couples and a changing cast of undergraduates who had big dangerous dogs and who did bonehead things like set their balconies on fire or drag their garbage to the dumpster through

the hallways and not bother to clean up the rotten eggs or cat litter that streamed from the broken bags. And then there were the
pot smells in the hallways and the empty beer cans on the lawn.

Maybe it was that one summer I went to Greece to research
olive groves that I came back to find that the city had passed a
referendum to fund a new middle school. It's likely I had voted
for it. I'd done artists-in-the-schools work at the middle school
and knew the current facility to be a horrendous tinderbox where
nobody could ever possibly learn anything. Certainly I wouldn't
begrudge the middle-schoolers a new building. But did they have
to build the thing on the most beautiful eastern rolling edge of
my meadow?

I should have remembered that I was a renter and not an
owner all along. And I suppose I should have known from the
very beginning that it was all business and not personal that first
day with Ed in the caddy, when we came back around the corner
after Ed showed me my apartment, and he confessed that he was
evicting the current tenants of the farmhouse he offered me on
the corner because they hadn't paid their rent in six months.

We drove by the intersection and watched them, sitting for-
lornly in the front yard of the farmhouse on their tumbling piles
of belongings like the Joads waiting for a truck to come and pick
them up. And when Ed asked if I wanted to stop and look inside
the farmhouse, I told him to keep going because I couldn't bear
to face someone else's misfortune on the top of my own sadness.

So I took the spacious three-bedroom apartment and bought
enough furniture to fill it, including a humongous princess-and-
pea king-size bed, which I still haven't slept on all the parts of,
even after nine years, and I made a studio overlooking the meadow where I managed to create a few good things, and I didn't
adopt a child, but instead created a library in the smallest bedroom, which for a long time I wouldn't refer to as a library, but
insisted on calling it "the room where I keep my books," until I
accepted that it was just easier to call it the library.

And my husband became my ex-husband but helped me move every stick and stitch of my belongings into the new place, because we agreed we would never allow ourselves to have that icky feeling upon parting. And when I started unpacking my books and putting them on my crappy old particle board book-shelves, he said, *No, I can't let you do that*, and he went out and bought me beautiful new bookshelves to put into my new library, which is one of the millions of reasons he remains my best friend in the world, even today.

And it was all hard to face—being alone those first months, where each minute of the weekend stretched on in infinite ticks of uncountable seconds, and the rooms were silent, and no phone rang. I moved into the apartment in August of 2001, and in September of that awful year, I was driving to the eastern part of Iowa for an event when the news broke about the towers falling in New York, and I circled back home and got into my big bed in that room where all the light comes in, and I watched CNN for hours, wondering if the world would ever be the same.

And in those rooms, I faced the reality that I'd never have children, and I came to realize that I had never really mourned the death of my father, so I sat on my off-white couch that first fall and cried for hours in shoulder-rocking spasms at the end of each day after coming home from teaching, and only the horses and the meadow bore witness.

I will acknowledge that in very recent history there must have been a farm where my own apartment building sits, and before that there was probably an oak savanna or a mixed-grass prairie, all of which were destroyed so that I could look at the meadow from these high windows. It seems we name things after what was destroyed to create them, which is why so little evidence of the Ioway tribe survives in Iowa, and also why we have treeless apartment complexes with names like Whispering Pines and Shady Acres, and housing developments with names like Hickory Grove Farms or Creekside Crossing, which is what they named the new strip of mini-mansions outside my windows.

The lone farmhouse and the falling-down outbuildings on the corner of South Dakota and Mortensen were razed soon after I moved into the neighborhood, and almost overnight three complexes of multi-story apartment buildings cropped up in the spot. So where once a single family lived rather inefficiently with a scraggly row of lilacs, now hundreds of people make their home with windows overlooking Highway 30 and the cornfields that stretch beyond it.

A big gas station lights up the opposite corner now—another Kum & Go—with a sports bar and a hot wings place behind it. And there are more apartment complexes beyond that with swimming pools and man-made ponds with squirting fountains in the center and even a workout place and a gourmet coffee shop, along with new bike paths that connect everything where the undeveloped acres used to be.

I'm not naïve. I know that life rushes forward and nothing stays put for very long. But for a time, there was a creek and an untended meadow behind my apartment where horses grazed. I faced the saddest days of my life in those rooms, and when it got really bad, worse than I ever imagined it would be, the sycamores lifted up their green arms to comfort me.

The Perils of Travel

Should we have stayed
at home and thought of here?

—Elizabeth Bishop, "Questions of Travel"

Something that unnerves me when I fly on certain Eastern European airlines is the way that passengers will applaud at touchdown, as if a crash landing were the norm, so an uneventful landing is a cause for celebration.

On most U.S. domestic flights, safe touchdowns are so thoroughly assumed that passengers are out of their seats, threading their arms through coat sleeves and eyeing the overhead compartments even as the plane's back tires screech down.

"Please stay in your seats," the cabin crew urges over the intercom. "The captain has not turned off the fasten seat belts sign!"

But on several European flights I've taken, conversation hushes at descent. Greeks, Cypriots, Russians sit up straight, look forward, spread their hands flat on their armrests. Are they thinking of loved ones or concentrating on keeping the plane in the air, as I am? And once we hear the concussion of the back tires on the tarmac, the cabin comes alive with applause. Passengers turn to each other and smile. They nod their heads at each other as if to say, "That was good, no? Again, we did not crash."

Perhaps I've imagined all this. Perhaps international flights are just traumatic for me, an American, because they remind me of how much farther away from home I'm taking myself, which forces the natural question—if I die abroad who will repatriate my body? Will it be my new boyfriend, my ex-husband, my mother, or some odd combination of all three working together? I imagine them collaborating, making travel plans on the phone after they've called each other to deliver the grim news of my demise. But how will they even find each other without my contacts list?

Will my ex-husband and my boyfriend travel together to pick up my body, my mother being too old and fearful of new places to go herself, and my new boyfriend being too new and too aggrieved to travel by himself? I imagine them sitting together on the flight—my new boyfriend and my ex-husband—two gorgeous dark-haired, dark-eyed men accepting their hot hand towels, their complimentary glasses of champagne, flirting, perhaps, with the flight attendant.

How dare they! And on the way to pick up my body. It makes me want to live, just to deprive them of the experience.

Americans are rather like bad Bulgarian wine:
they don't travel well.
          —Bernard Falk

Some travelers, I have observed, take the earliest opportunity to imperil themselves when they arrive at their destinations. The bag is barely unpacked before they must climb the highest bell tower or ride the shaky tram suspended by frayed cables to the peak of the nearest mountain. They must take the creaking elevator to the top of the Eiffel Tower, or huff up the three-hundred-odd steps, cobbled together in the sixteenth century, we are assured, by the finest of Europe's masons, to the lean tip of the ancient cathedral.

They must stand in the crumbling eye of the wind-blown spire and, if that's not enough, step out onto the shaky platform with no guard-rails. I've never had such a desire when traveling.

On my first trip to Paris, I unwittingly enlisted myself in a perilous adventure with Steven, a fellow American I met at my hotel, the Grand Hotel Des Balcons. I suppose it was the sadness I observed in him each morning as he ate his fifty-franc breakfast breakfast, cracking his hard-boiled egg, spooning his yogurt so thoughtfully, and reading a book in English, I noticed, which first made me aware that he was likely an American.

When I saw him days later, walking along the rue Casimir-Delavigne with that same English novel tucked under the sleeve of his brown corduroy jacket, I felt compelled to stop him and introduce myself. We talked like old friends on that windy street, just off the busy St-Germain-des-Pres, and discovered that we were both writers—he, from the West Coast; me, from the Midwest.

In minutes, we disclosed a great deal about ourselves, as travelers and Americans tend to do, and especially as traveling Americans do. I liked him immediately and found it a relief to speak to someone in fluent English after ten days by myself in Paris during which time I had communicated mostly with hand gestures, exaggerated facial movements, and confusing English fragments, which I delivered in what I thought to be a French accent. I don't know why I began speaking broken English with a French accent as soon as I arrived in Paris. But it only seemed that my English was better understood when I did so.

Talking with Steven on the sidewalk outside our hotel, it seemed exhilarating to be gushing English to someone and to have someone gushing English back to me. I liked him, but I wasn't attracted to him. Not in that way you imagine you might someday be attracted to someone you meet when you're traveling and unsupervised, in that no-one's-watching-anyway, one-night-stand kind of way. His hair seemed too neatly combed, I think, his clothes too uniform. Plus, there was this business of his over-whelming sadness.

Even though he smiled a great deal as he told me that he was treating himself to this trip to Paris as a reward for completing his first novel, he did not seem to be a man who was celebrat-ing. Soon I discovered the reason—he was newly divorced, had a young daughter whom he missed terribly, and, to add insult to injury, his newly divorced wife was a quite famous novelist. I pretended to be impressed when he told me her name, but really it only made me feel more sad for him.

He told me that the next day would be his final day in Paris, and that he had planned to visit the Catacombs buried under the city of Paris, then finish off the day with dinner at The Proco-pe, an upscale restaurant in Paris that bore the distinction—or at least claimed to bear the distinction—of being the oldest eating establishment in all of Europe.

As if on impulse, Steven asked me if I'd like to spend the next day with him, and just as impulsively, I said yes.

There is no greater bore than a travel bore. We do not in the least want to hear what he has seen in Hong Kong.
—Vita Sackville-West

The next morning after breakfast, Steven and I set out in good walking shoes with our water bottles and backpacks. As we climbed above ground from the Denfert-Rochereau Metro stop, we walked a bit before coming upon the entrance to the Cata-combs on the edge of the 14th arrondissement.

I had traveled to Paris to find some traces of my immigrant family's original culture. Even though my family had emigrated from France to Russia in the early 1800s, and then to America in the early 1900s, I still felt, as I walked the streets of Paris, an affinity—the food, the smells, a gesture, the curve of a cheekbone, the angle of an eye. I saw my brother, my father, my sisters each day as I walked down the streets. Given that between five to six million people had been buried in the Catacombs over the course of the last two centuries, I thought it would be as close to visiting a family grave as I would get while visiting France.

Steven and I waited in the long queue forming outside the entrance. At 11:00 a.m., the doors flung open and the line began to move. To my right as we filed quickly through the lobby, I noticed a map mounted on the wall showing the cavern we were to enter—1.5 miles of underground walkways full of bones. The Reliquary tunnels, I had read in the guidebooks, were created in the twelfth and thirteenth centuries out of the giant caverns that resulted from quarrying the limestone that was used for buildings, churches, ramparts, and monuments all around the city of Paris.

The first burials in the Catacombs were necessitated by health concerns during massive plague outbreaks in the 1780s. The numerous skeletons were dismantled, reorganized by part, and interred below in neat piles of skulls, femurs, fibulas, and tibias. Death, the great leveler. As one guidebook announced, no distinction for class or political persuasion was made here, "The skull of a revolutionary may be resting on the leg of an aristocrat; noble and corrupt, young and old, wealthy and poor, all are indistinguishable now."

As we waited in line, I had some horror-movie imaginings of what we would find below—shelves of laughing jaw bones, long bony-fingered hands, heaping piles of yellow, clacking teeth. The guidebook said the Reliquary was dark, and the crypt floor was covered with lime. The book advised to wear good shoes and bring a flashlight. Always the careful traveler, I had packed two flashlights and a compass.

At the Catacomb entrance, Steven and I were pulled by the momentum of the crowd through an area cordoned off with red velvet ropes. We threw our thirty-five francs each at the woman behind the plate glass window and dashed to the right where a man in a red suit pointed to a slim descending staircase straight ahead.

Down we went, following those ahead of us. The stairs were narrow, just room enough for one person, and they curved downward in tight 360-degree revolutions. I took one complete circle down the staircase, then another. The people in front of me tramped ahead briskly; I matched their pace. The people behind us pushed and moved as we moved. We were descending deeper, making one revolution down then another when my feet began to go numb.

My lungs grew heavy in my chest. I halted in mid-step and grasped the handrail. The people ahead of me on the staircase rushed headlong, disappearing down and down the spiral into the cavern. An emptiness opened beneath me on the staircase. I could feel Steven's weight behind me and all the weight of anxious tourists that accumulated up the steps behind him—everyone mad to get underground and see the famous cache of bones.

"There's no one coming up." I whispered, as if I'd uncovered a government conspiracy—France's solution to the problem of too many American tourists?

"Steven," I said, "this staircase only goes one way."

"What?" Steven asked. His voice was strained and breathless.

"I can't go another step." I sobbed.

"Oh my God," Steven said with alarm. "Are you claustrophobic?"

"I don't think so," I said. Then I realized I, really, sort of, was. I don't like elevators or crowded rooms or basements without windows. Now I recalled the passing glimpse I'd taken of the Catacomb map on the wall. The red dotted line marking the underground walking path—1.5 miles—that would finally deliver you to the exit. I realized this was all a one-way trip.

"Oh my God," Steven repeated, realizing the situation. "One time I was in the middle of the Golden Gate Bridge, and my feet stopped moving just like this."

He was saying this to comfort me, but the image of being stranded in the middle of the Golden Gate Bridge didn't help.

In fact, it made me begin to hyperventilate, since I'm even more afraid of water and heights than I am of small spaces.

I should have known better than to attempt the Catacombs, but they were a common tourist attraction, all the guidebooks said so. Every year thousands of families—teenagers, infants, toddlers, parents—rolled down this staircase in their khaki shorts and Planet Hollywood t-shirts to take a gander at the acres of dismembered skeletons. This cavern has been in use for over seven hundred years—revolutionaries, bandits, peasants, workers going in and out at all times of the day and night.

It takes supreme arrogance, I realize, to believe that the day you choose to visit the Catacombs, the eight-hundred-year-old cavern will decide to give way and bury you and all the unfortunate other people who descended with you on that day. It goes along with being Catholic, I think, the belief that the very particular finger of God is always on just you.

I'm also certain the centuries-old smoldering volcano will blow the very day I visit; I know the hook-echo of the tornado is heading for my front door. I wouldn't risk the observation decks of either the Space Needle or the leaning tower of Pisa, nor would I linger around the Acropolis too long, lest the ancient ruins decided to become completely ruined on the day that I visit.

Now that I was frozen on the Catacombs staircase, there was no arguing with my body. I tossed the flashlights and compass in Steven's direction and grabbed the banister. "Go on without me." I threw my shoulder like a wedge into the dozens of tourists pressed behind him, and I began to scale the stairs.

"But where will you be?" Steven asked as I moved past him.

"I'll find you," I shouted back, "wherever you exit." It sounded dramatic, even as I said it, like when Daniel Day Lewis yelled to Madeleine Stowe in *The Last of the Mohicans* as she was being abducted by unfriendly Apaches, "Stay alive, no matter how long it takes, I will find you."

Steven grew smaller and smaller as I climbed higher. "Tell me everything you see," I yelled, pulling myself up like a salmon swimming against the current. The going was slow.

People muttered in every imaginable language as I squeezed past them. I apologized my way up the curving handrail, *ex-cus-e-moi-ing* and pardon-me-ing as I climbed. When I reached the ground-level opening, the people waiting to descend parted for me to climb out. Without a word, the man in the red suit opened a velvet rope that led to a side exit. He didn't look surprised; I suspected this happened more than a few times a day.

I circled around to the front and swam through the crowd to have one quick look at the map in the lobby that listed a street-level exit point several blocks away called the Ossuary Exit. The word, *ossuary*, with its close association to *ossifying* and *ossification* made me shiver. I had a palpable moment of claustrophobia even then, just imagining myself gasping for breath, trapped in that underground cavern as it collapsed around me. I sprang out of the front door of the Reliquary entrance, driven by the strong impulse to breathe and be supple in my limbs.

Outside, it was a cool, summer morning, not even noon yet. It felt good to breathe in the clear air, the sunlight shining hot on my face. I wandered for blocks in this new light and open space, elated with my good fortune for being this very breathing, above-ground being.

> *Travel is glamorous, only in retrospect.*
> —Paul Theroux

I wound up on a grassy berm somewhere near the boulevard du Montparnasse where so many American writers have sat in smoky cafés and discussed great, developing works of art. The lawn felt so green and open-air against my skin that it was hard to believe that tourists were paying money to walk underground and view the ancient bones of by-gone Parisians.

I walked a few more blocks finding only unfamiliar street names. I began to worry. In his backpack, Steven carried the guidebooks and the map back to the hotel. He had navigated us here on the Metro. I had no good idea of where in the city we were.

Ahead of me on the boulevard, I saw three women approaching. I resolved to ask them for help, and I prepared myself for a rebuff. In my experience, men all over Europe will help a single woman. A woman traveling alone seems to be an affront to European men. If you are lost, they will offer to walk you to your destination. If you are eating alone, they will insist you join their group at dinner; they will pour you wine from their carafes, offer cigarettes and matches to light them, then invite you to come along for drinks or a coffee afterwards.

Struggling with my bags in European train stations, I have had men pick up my heaviest suitcase, carry it onto the train for me, and go on their way without a word. The friends to whom I've expressed this observation say cynically that the men were simply trying to pick me up. This may be sometimes true, but I don't believe it is always so.

For the most part, I've observed a civility in Europeans that Americans do not possess. Lost in a large American city, I expect and hope to be left alone, to flounder in my lost and aloneness. In Europe, I know I will be helped. But my observation has also been that European women are less friendly and helpful; just as, in America, I am less likely to help strangers. This is perhaps true all over the world because women must be more mindful of their personal security.

"Pardon me," I said to the three approaching women. They were French, each one more tall, slim, and angular than the next. "Can you tell me where is the Ossuary Exit?" In my broken English with a fake French accent, it sounded like a bizarre question.

"Ah, an American," one of the women said with excitement. She fell on me and grabbed my arm as if I were her sister.

"Yes," I conceded. Usually I tried to conceal my American-ness, even declaring myself a Canadian if times got desperate, and speaking with crisper enunciation and emphasizing my higher, rounder vowels, which I got from growing up in a high, northern state. When I travel, I try to dress well, refusing to wear the typical American tourist costume—tennis shoes, khaki shorts and an untucked t-shirt with a logo from some garish American franchise like the Hard Rock Café. I find the better dressed I am when I travel, the better I am treated by everyone I encounter.

Now I spoke in English to the three French women, who listened attentively. I spilled it all out—about the Catacombs, my panic, my surprise at my claustrophobia. The most friendly woman seemed to have the best English. She held my forearm as I talked. All three "No'd" and "Yes'd" through my story, then they had a short interchange in French. They talked quickly, nodded, and clicked their tongues; they didn't need to translate. *The Catacombs, yes, a ghastly place.*

They were beautiful women, long-limbed and elegant. They walked six blocks out of their way to show me to the Ossuary Exit, then the friendliest one kissed both my cheeks and deposited me on the dusty stoop overlooking the opening.

I sat on the curb after they left, drinking a bottle of mineral water, and watching as countless tourists ascended the steps from the Catacombs. Many of them came through the Ossuary Exit, short of breath and perspiring. They emptied out onto the sidewalk, many of them ashen, bending over, taking deep gulps of air as they stepped into the light.

You could see that the journey through the cavern had been an ordeal for them, as I suspected it would be. But when, I wondered, had it occurred to them that danger was possible or imminent—somewhere deep underground, when it was too late? Either I was too phobia-laden and full of trepidation to be a truly intrepid traveler, or I had an early-warning system programmed into my DNA, the same thing that impelled my ancestors to flee revolutions in France, then Russia.

My family line had survived, after all, because my ancestors had known to read the early warning signs and flee the instability of Alsace in 1803. Their descendants had known to pick up stakes and flee the growing instability of Russia one hundred years later. Even as a wild young woman in 1960s America, seemingly racing toward the brink of destruction, I always knew before my friends when to put on the brakes.

> *Far travel, very far travel, or travail, comes near to the worth*
> *of staying at home.*
> —Henry David Thoreau

Steven appeared eventually up the Catacomb steps. He was happy and perspiring, but not traumatized in any way from his journey through the underworld.

True to his word, he told me everything he had seen as we walked back to the Metro stop—the long, dark tunnels, the dripping water, the bone heaps, piles of craniums, the walls of bones quilted with patterns of femurs, and, near the end of the trek, the clear water drinking fountain of Lethe, or *de l'oublie*, which invites you to drink and forget all that you have seen on your passage. Showing the greatest restraint and good taste, Steven did not ask me about my panic on the stairs or question me about my claustrophobia.

Later that night, after I bathed and put on a fresh, black dress and sandals, I met him in the hotel lobby and we walked the few blocks in the Latin Quarter to the Procope. The food was good as I recall—oysters on the half shell with mignonnette sauce, brazed duck with glazed shallots, chocolate souffle for dessert—but the waiters glared at us with the delivery of each platter.

In between courses, we licked our wounds by making fun of the scowling waiter, deciding that even though The Procope boasted the longest run as any eating establishment in Europe, they still had not perfected their style. In all the meals I had in Paris, before or since, it was the only one in which I was treated badly.

Steven insisted on paying for the meal, the price of which I knew was exorbitant. We walked back to the hotel in silence. It was his last night in Paris. We collected our keys at the hotel desk under the suspicious eye of the clerk and walked together up the spiral staircase of the Hotel des Balcons.

I recall inviting him into my room for a moment, because it seemed rude not to do so, even though I didn't have any wine or coffee or cognac and chocolates to offer him. He sat on the edge of my bed for a time, and we talked about writing. He talked about his early flight, calculating how much time he should allow for getting to the airport in the morning. And then he left, perhaps seeing that I was not interested in anything more than talk.

At the doorway, we double-kissed each other's cheeks and exchanged business cards. We promised to e-mail, but we never did. In the years since, I've looked for his published novel, putting his name into the search engine of Amazon from time to time. As far as I can tell, his novel has never appeared, although his ex-wife, I have observed, continues to get more and more famous with each passing year.

Odessa!

Whenever I've been to Russia, I can't wait to get away.
Then I can't wait to get back.

—Bruce Chatwin

As a child, I was a map-gazer. I'd set my small finger down in Alsace, in that blessed valley of castles, church spires, vineyards, and rolling fields of sunflowers between the Vosges Mountains and the Rhine river from which my ancestors originated, then I'd tramp my fingers like a small scissors eastward through Germany. I'd touch down on the shore of the Danube and trace its long artery, the eastern route my people took to reach Odessa on the Black Sea in 1803. I longed to feel under my fingertips the slow progress of the overland caravan, the teams of oxen, the pots and pans, the crying babies—a 1,900-mile journey—just to reach the acres of unbroken steppe land near the Black Sea that had been offered to my ancestors by Czar Alexander I.

Odessa! Just the name conjured images. I was growing up in Napoleon, a small town near Bismarck, equally evocative names, but Odessa sounded to me like destination number one—poor Odysseus trying and not trying to make it home from the Trojan

Wars. And the Black Sea, which was nothing like the Red Sea or the Dead Sea, but black, meaning danger, the unknown. I admired the mettle of my ancestors. They had walked through the Black Forest to get to the Black Sea.

My own grandparents had no detailed memories of Eastern Europe—my maternal and paternal grandfathers fled Russia as children to come to the Dakota Territory with their parents, in 1886 and 1911, respectively. Still, when they died, Odessa was listed as the place of birth on all their funeral cards, and as they died one by one, something of the exotic went with them.

And so it is with loss: eventually all one is left with is words. So it happened that in 1998, I decided to retrace my ancestors' route across Eastern Europe—first, under the power of Lufthansa from Munich to Vienna, then after a brief passport check, on to Odessa via Austrian Airlines. With 747s and Visa cards, I would do in five and a half hours what it had taken my ancestors four arduous months and countless deaths along the way to accomplish in 1803.

I wrote the grants, made all the arrangements for the eight-week trek that would take me first to the *ville natale*, my ancestors' original villages in the Rhine region of France, then on to the Ukraine and parts of Russia. By mid-August, I should be in Novosibirsk in western Siberia. I intended to scour the planet, or at least selected parts of Central and Eastern Europe, for lost landscapes, lost stories, lost cousins.

This had all sounded like great fun in January, but standing in the Des Moines International Airport on July 7, as my husband walked me to the departing gate, I was struck with the enormity of the task I had dreamed up for myself. I panicked as he pushed me through the gate at the last possible call. I pulled at his sleeve. "Please don't send me to Siberia," I blubbered, and we both started to laugh. Already Russia was starting to have its crazy effect on me.

At the moment of touchdown in Odessa, as it turns out, I was not surprised or worried or gazing in wonder (as my older cousin, Lew, had told me to do) at the aerial view of the Kutschurgan Liman, the place where the Dniester River widens into a lagoon before emptying into the Black Sea. Instead, I was flirting shamelessly with a muscular, gold-skinned Austrian Airlines Security officer—whose name, I swear to God, was Hans—who had many empty seats to choose from at the beginning of the flight, but who chose the empty seat next to mine to sit in.

Over Bratislava, Hans and I had exchanged pleasantries; we balanced our plates of chicken Kiev over Budapest and spoke of his weightlifting regimen over Romania. How gorgeous he was in his regulation short-sleeved white shirt. Across the entire Czech Republic, we shared an arm rest—the hair of his arm brushing against my skin, my small tan forearm so close to his muscular bicep. By the time we reached Moldova, he was translating my horoscope from a German newspaper. Adventure and romance were in my future, he said, then he read his own horoscope in silence with a slight smile on his face.

Upon descent he told me in the most adorable Austrian accent that it was his job to re-escort any passengers back to Vienna who did not have proper visas. I reached for my papers wishing I had not chosen the very thorough Seattle-based travel agency, Mir Corporation, to make all my eastern European arrangements. I watched over his magnificent shoulder as he scanned my visa, hoping for an uncrossed t, an undotted i. But no, he handed them back to me with a sad look, everything was in fine order. The bumblers and the incompetents would go back to Vienna with Hans, but I would be staying in Odessa.

Perhaps it's best to begin with my shoes—Simples—the tan, suede walking shoes that were on my feet the spring day, a year earlier, when I sat on the shore of Lake Superior and dreamed up this Russia excursion. On the rubber sole of Simples is an arrow under the big toe pointing forward. By the forward arrow are the words, "the future." There's another arrow, under the heel, pointing backwards, and the words beside it read, "the past." Under the arch of the foot, that delicate part that does not touch down, the rubber sole says, "Simple." But is it?

The future's ahead of you; walk forward to find it. The past is behind you; remember it. But the present, this small space that is supported by a tenuous curving arch, is suspended between the future and the past. This is your present, your small spot on earth. Each time you set your foot down, you make your path. The past may have claims on you; the future will make demands, but this small space under the arch, this is yours to do with as you wish. I get philosophical like this when I get around Lake Superior.

Superior and I have an agreement. I make a pilgrimage to it yearly; it doesn't care. I confess all; it doesn't listen. Every word and sadness I deposit on its shore sinks to its coldest depths; it doesn't feel the weight or passage of my troubles. Superior is old, older than caring. This omnipotent obliviousness comforts me.

Since my father died one year earlier, I'd dragged several unwieldy deposits of grief to it like sharp boulders in canvas sacks. For all that effort, I still carried a permanent medium-sized rock in my throat and a large stone in my belly. What is the shape and size of grief? What is its longest possible duration? It is large and full of heaviness; it is old as the half-life of refined uranium.

Geologists believe Lake Superior exists because the continent tried to split down the center millions of years ago. The tear that was left behind became Superior once the glacial ice receded, depositing one-tenth of the world's freshwater supply in the crevice. I am drawn to the drama of that kind of geological violence, to the beauty that violence renders on a landscape.

That summer, I felt my own life to be straddling two splitting halves of a once-solid continent. I was forty-two years old, still childless, but now trying to have a child; all my grandparents were dead, and now my father was gone. Sharon Olds says about her maturing daughter in one of her poems: "It's the oldest story; the story of replacement." The past of my childhood, an entire generation of sausage-making, polka-dancing people had all but disappeared; the future, the smooth-headed replacements, were not forthcoming. The horizon seemed suddenly empty. Most days, I felt like an actor in one of those post-apocalyptic movies, walking across a dry unpopulated landscape, calling, calling.

That spring morning, I sat on a bench near the boardwalk of Lake Superior. I'd gone there early to be with the lake before the joggers and the dog-walkers. The lake neither approved of nor disliked this practice, but it pleased me. A Russian tanker, the *Goviken*, was floating about a mile offshore. I watched its craggy profile in the distance. The *Goviken* was waiting, I was told the day before while on a tour of the Duluth Seaway Port Authority, for the price of wheat to go down by a few cents. When this happened, it would spin its engines, blow its horn, and come through the channel.

Once inside the harbor, it would center itself in the water below one of the many loading spigots and fill its belly with wheat. When full, it would exit the channel and slink past the other great lakes, through the lock system along the St. Lawrence Seaway, wide-bottomed and heavy with grain, back to St. Petersburg.

If I had been thinking of wheat that morning it may have struck me as ironic that my family's wheat, which for over a hundred years has been shipped to this port in Duluth across the plains via the Northern Pacific railroad, would be making a second migration I had not imagined to all parts of the world—India, England, Vietnam. Those were the various destinations of the wheat-seeking salties, the sea-bearing vessels, when I'd looked in the Port Authority logbook on the tour the day before.

It was entirely possible that tomorrow or the next day some of my family's wheat would go into the *Goviken*, to be returned to Russia. This seemed especially sad, since my great-grandfather fled Russia in 1886 and took up a land claim in Dakota Territory, only to grow hard Durham wheat, Russian wheat, on the Dakota plains and have it be returned to Russia. I get dizzy thinking of it, the political migrations of wheat. Would it not have been more efficient for my great-grandfather to have stayed in Russia, raised Russian wheat on Russian soil to be distributed in Russia? By all reports, his whole life he carried a nostalgia for the place and wished for the chance to return if only the political climate would improve. Of course, it never did. Not in his lifetime.

But I was not thinking of wheat that day; I was thinking of eggs. My own, which I had recently learned were becoming rarer and more corrupted by the hour. I was trying to give this sadness over to the lake, as I sat on the boardwalk bench in a yoga position with the rubber lug soles of my Simples touching. I was stretching my thigh muscles, thinking about the conversation I'd had with a doctor about my poor, corrupted eggs just before I'd left home for Superior. This was not my doctor, but a specialist who was so special that it had taken many tiers of climbing, many referrals and office visits to less special specialists—my PCP, and my regular speculum-wielding OB-GYN, until I found myself, as if granted an audience with the Pope, in the presence of Dr. Swanson, the fertility specialist.

For weeks, by proxy and underlings, Dr. Swanson had been ordering lab tests for me. My trips to the clinic to draw blood were made between classes and appointments. First thing in the morning, all for Dr. Swanson's benefit, I tracked my temperature using a basal thermometer. I noted the onset and duration of my period, and I recorded all this information with dots on a little grid he had provided in a pre-appointment packet. At the end of the month, I drew my own line through thirty days of daily temperatures that showed my rising and falling fertility fortunes. It looked like a financial analysis grid for the Dow Jones Industrial Average.

The charts now sat before Dr. Swanson, along with my growing file—reports from all the lesser doctors, and my lab results. Dr. Swanson was a busy man; he came right to the point. When he matched my FSH and Estradiol levels against my temperatures, which indicated my days of ovulation, he could see immediately that I was unlikely to achieve a pregnancy. He said all of this matter-of-factly, without looking up at me. It was clear that he had studied all of my numbers ahead of time, particularly my age, and made the decision that I was simply a fool. What had I been thinking?

I sat quietly in the bright white office looking at Dr. Swanson as he delivered the news—his clicking, silver pen, his deep tan. Remember this, I thought. Here is a moment, not like any other.

My silence caught Dr. Swanson's attention. He looked up at me, sitting in the extra chair in his exam room, crestfallen, on the verge of tears. He looked at me again, then flipped the chart forward to double-check my age. He looked at me; he looked at the chart. Did he have the wrong chart? Was I really this patient, a forty-two-year-old white woman named Debra? Yes, I said. He exhaled in a long whistle and complimented me on how gracefully I was aging.

"Tell that to my ovaries," I said. He laughed and something easy broke between us.

Dr. Swanson pulled off his glasses and brought them to his lap. "Of course you can always buy whatever you don't have," he said. Here was insider information. He was going the extra mile for me. "Sperm, eggs, a uterus."

When I assured him I had no intention of doing anything high-tech or invasive, I saw disappointment pass over Dr. Swanson's face. He was the wizard and I had ordered the magic show stopped.

"Just as well," he said, after I dismissed the possibility of in vitro fertilization. "In a case like yours," he said, "you'd have to throw a lot of sperm at the problem."

Of course, I understood what he meant—it would be rigorous, disappointing, and expensive with very little chance of a positive outcome. But the only thing I could think of was—how did I get in this position? I was a woman after all, who had been offered great quantities of sperm in my twenties and thirties. In my pelvis, I had carried a glowing purse of eggs. Everywhere I went—the office, the grocery store, the gas station—men had tried to throw sperm at me. Sometimes I accepted; most times I did not. To be democratic, I turned away more than I took. And to think I had squandered so much sperm, when I could have collected it in jars by my bed and set to work with a turkey baster. I wouldn't need Dr. Swanson; I could have been my own home fertility experiment.

And how did it happen that all those fast-talking, backstroking, streetwise sperm had been outfoxed by my evasive maneuvers, all my chemical shields, leaving the gold clasp of the treasure chest undone? We had been elitists and snobs, I realized now, overly vigilant—me and my golden eggs—looking down our noses at the multitudes of common sperm, as if they were the extras, the cast of thousands in *Ben Hur*.

Now sperm was suddenly precious. It was the star of the show, the billion-footed savior riding in legion to salvage the situation, while my eggs were a vain, aging film actress with her face lifts and head scarves who still thinks she can play the ingenue.

"I only thought," I continued meekly, "that you might be able to give me something to boost my fertility levels, to increase the possibility of pregnancy."

Dr. Swanson lowered his eyes, shaking his head at my naïve suggestion, as if I had requested magic beans. "I can tell you," he said, "that women in your situation, if they get pregnant will only do so spontaneously."

Spontaneously. This word surprised me—the inaccuracy of its use in this context of precise charts and mathematical formulas. Dr. Swanson went on to explain that his older patients in my hormonal situation, when they got pregnant, had gotten pregnant spontaneously (naturally, he explained). Now I understood, but the word *spontaneously* would not leave my imagination. I thought of those paintings of the Virgin Mary full of gold light by Van Eyck or some other master of the Renaissance—the immaculate conception. A gold ray of light shines on you through the rafters and whoops, spontaneous pregnancy.

I thought of the description of impregnation in Aborigine culture in Robert Lawlor's *Voices of the First Day*. An Aborigine woman is walking along a path. She might be gathering berries or drawing water, and whoops, her womb quickens—sometimes it feels like a tiny bite—and spontaneously she knows she's pregnant. Lawlor reports that the woman then rushes to the village elders, who return with her to the spot where she felt the tremor. By its location, they will determine which natural element or force of nature fathered the child.

Was it such a surprise then that I was sitting in the lotus position on the shore of Lake Superior offering my loins to one-tenth of the world's freshwater supply? Never mind; biology had had its day.

I shifted my shoes and studied the arrows—the future expects you to find it. Biologically, I had no future. But I had more than sixteen doses of the past to draw from. I had knowledge of six grandfathers named Joseph, going back in time as if riding on each other's shoulders like a totem pole. They had spread their bodies from Alsace to Odessa to the Dakota Territory over the last two centuries, just so I could sit here at this moment.

In my hometown on Halloween, we would scour the houses in town for candy. And before we could have the candy, the question would always come: "And who do you belong to?" All we had to do was lift our masks and people would say, "Oh, it's Felix's kids." Now there was no Felix, and there was not even a person with candy behind the door to ask the question. Everyone who would know and remember me was gone. If there would be no line going out of me to the future, I would have to find my tribe elsewhere. I would have to march backwards into Russia and bang my fists on vine-covered doors. Someone would have to claim me as their own.

The Taste of Home

At the Bismarck Airport, I pick up the jar of chokecherry jelly in the gift shop before boarding my flight back to Iowa. Not sure when I'll make it home to North Dakota again.

I stash the jar in my kitchen pantry, waiting for the right time to open it—maybe at the end of summer, the time of most longing, when I remember how we walked dusty rows through slants of sunlight to harvest the berries so that Mom could colander the pits away from the fruit, bubble it on the stove top with sugar, and transform chokecherries into jars of jam (thicker) and syrup (thinner), each sealed with a hardened layer of poured wax on top.

The thought of chokecherries brings with it my mother's overnight buns. Roll out of bed at first light and follow the yeasty sweetness down to the kitchen. Grab a palm-scorching bun straight out of the oven and puncture one teeny, tiny hole in the side—small enough to preserve the heat but large enough to wedge in a slab of butter and a spoonful of chokecherry jam. Pinch the teeny, tiny hole closed and wait—one, two, three, four— then bite into the out-of-the-oven doughy sweetness along with the lava flow of molten butter co-mingled with bitter drippings of chokecherry. That's winter.

Chokecherry is bright and berry-like in the front of the mouth, but when it migrates to the back of the tongue it digs into the tastebuds and expands into small peppery pods of semi-bitterness. This must be the "chokey" part, the reason for the name. Not pinkish-red and full of seeds like raspberry jam or deep maroon like boysenberry, chokecherry jam is bright magenta in the jar but turns a muted mauve in the bowl when it's mixed with melting ice cream or swirled into a thin layer of heavy cream, as we used to eat it, and sopped up with fresh bread—a dish we German-Russians called *dungus*. Don't bother to inquire who first thought to make this dish or calculate the fat and calorie content. This is summer.

Summer or winter at home in Napoleon, the largely German-Russian town where I grew up, there were always dumplings (potatoes and onions frying under steaming pillows of dough; don't open the cover or they'll all collapse), and *halupsy* (a mixture of ground beef with tomatoes rolled in beds of cabbage leaves), and *kuchen* (a doughy crust with sweet custard filling and a tart topping surprise of prunes). Who knew prunes could ever be good?

The taste of home is confusing like this. Take *plachinda*—pie crust rolled into circles to make small finger-cinched half-moon pockets with a pumpkin filling seasoned with nutmeg, cinnamon, sometimes cloves, plus minced onion, sugar, salt and pepper. Sweet, salty, and savory!

If I close my eyes, I am still there, sitting in the basement of my maternal grandparents' house in town where they lived after they moved in from the farm, and my grandpa Geist is feeding a salted and seasoned ground pork and beef mixture into filmy streams of thin intestines to make his own homemade sausage, which still, in my memory, tastes better (and I know this is sacrilege) than Wishek sausage—a local delicacy made at Stan's Supermarket in Wishek that is so smoke-seasoned to perfection that people travel from all parts with empty coolers just to fill up on their year's supply of Wishek sausage: Liver, Summer, Ring Bologna, and Country Style.

And speaking of proliferations of forms. Can we talk about *knoephla?* How many ways can this dish be eaten? Start with the basic ball of dough, then snip off pieces with a scissors into little fleshy triangles. After that, do you fry them up in the pan with onions and add sauerkraut and homemade Wishek sausage? Do you drop them in a potato-onion-broth base with cream and make knoephla soup? Or do you roll the dough flat, cut it into squares, and lay down dollops of eggy cottage cheese in each one, then pinch together to make little wedged pockets of deliciousness called case knoephla (sometimes known as "cheese buttons")? There is no wrong answer. All of the above.

My sister Judy, before her death, ran a small cottage industry of knoephla-making out of her home kitchen, which was always an assembly line of flour sifting and batch making. Late into the night after she came home from her real job, she'd stand at the island counter in her kitchen and measure, knead, roll, and weigh the dough into mounds, then snip, snip, snip the knoephla into plastic freezer baggies and sell them, fresh or frozen, to everyone across south central North Dakota.

The recipe is simple enough. Flour, salt, egg, water, in some mysterious combination. But Judy had the trick of it, everyone agreed. People came to her door, called her on the phone. *Can you bring me four bags of knoephla, I have company coming. Can I buy six bags, I'll throw them in the freezer.* What was her secret?

One night while I was visiting, after I kept her company while she made batch after batch of knoephla, we retreated to the living room where she sat down, flour-dusted from head to toe, lit a smoke, and popped open a Budweiser. After some talk, she leaned over and pulled a pen and small pad of paper out of her end table drawer and jotted down her recipe for knoephla—the keys to the kingdom on a small piece of paper, which I promptly misplaced in my many piles of paper back in Iowa.

My sister's death was unexpected. When we gathered at her memorial service, people spoke with awe and longing about her food—some of them still had bags of her knoephla in their freezers, some bemoaned that she had taken her mysteriously good recipe for potato salad to the grave.

Did I mention to any of these people that she had bequeathed to me her knoephla recipe? I did not. I now jealously guard it like some people hold close the location of the best trout fishing spot in the river, or the most prodigious morel patch in the woods.

The book of Corinthians says we must put away childish things, but let's agree not to do that with food. What good can come from giving up Dots, for example.

For years, I have argued that Dots are the perfect food. Vegan, kosher, and gluten-free. What more can you ask of a food? Soft gumdrop morsels of cherry, strawberry, lemon, lime, and orange. (Strike from your mind the candy maker's unfortunate "improvisations" on a perfect thing: Sour Dots, Tropical Dots, Yogurt Dots. Just, *yuck*.)

But "Original" Dots are perfect—if a movie makes you nervous, you can occupy yourself by flattening Dots between your thumb and index finger and feed them to yourself like sweet coins into a slot machine, or you can cluster-pop four and five of them straight into your mouth. When chewed, Dots leave behind trace amounts of themselves in your gums and the crevices of your teeth, to be worked out later—the afterglow, the treat that keeps on giving!

As candy goes, Dots are the most efficient delivery method of high fructose corn syrup to the body. The shortest distance between tongue and bloodstream.

I don't associate Dots with childhood, specifically, although I'm sure I first tasted them at the movie theater in my hometown, along with salty popcorn and butterfingers and walnut crushes. But I've carried Dots through my adult life, always making sure to have a movie-theater-sized box stashed somewhere in my kitchen (okay, the corner cabinet to the right of the stove) or in the cubbyhole of my car.

It was my love of Dots that led me to discover another taste from home that has crowded itself to the top of my home foods pantheon: Dot's Homestyle Pretzels.

A few years ago, while traveling around western North Dakota, I was in a truck stop outside of Williston stocking up on road food. Because I've spent so much of my life on the road (in the '70s and '80s I was a road musician), I feel I'm uniquely qualified to recommend my six or seven top road foods: beyond coffee and a water bottle, you should carry Gatorade (orange or fruit punch), Caramellos, beef jerky, Tootsie Rolls, Corn Nuts (ranch flavor), and Almond Joys (such restraint   just the one perfect almond floating in the center of all that chocolate-covered coconut!).

At the gas station outside Williston, I asked the cashier where I might find Dots, and she pointed me to a stand-alone kiosk at the end of the aisle stocked to the gills with jumbo bags of Dot's Homestyle Pretzels. For the first time, I saw that fiery red font superimposed over what appears to be an entire room full of golden twist pretzels, with highlights of cayenne red flashing along the edges and the "Pride of North Dakota" decal displayed prominently in the top right corner of the package.

I hesitated—can one road trip sustain two kinds of Dot's? Sweet Dot's and savory Dot's. Would this constitute Dot's infidelity?

On the road in western North Dakota that winter, I consumed my first bag of Dot's Homestyle Pretzels, and I haven't looked back since, except to search for them in stores every time I come back to North Dakota.

Dot's Pretzels' website describes them as "the snack you didn't know you needed," and a truer statement was never uttered. Sometimes you eat something that just feels so familiar. Not like "Grandma made these and I love them," but more like "by God, my soul needed this." Dot's Pretzels are like this—at once, they taste new and surprising to the tongue, but ancient and primal to the brain.

Rip open a bag of Dot's Pretzels and lean in. The first thing you smell is butter. The ingredient label promises that it is "artificial butter flavor," but my nose reads "real." Reach in, and your fingers come away with a light dusting of the topping (to be lip-smacked later). The first bite brings with it the buttery crunch of the pretzel and saltiness, but not too much.

Then something richer hunkers down toward the back of the mouth, something more complicated. What is it? The label promises buttermilk salt. I fed them to a friend who is a food scientist and she tasted nutritional yeast, which has a subtle nutty-cheesy (but not salty) aftertaste. My partner, Tom, tastes garlic and garlic salt in the mix. I taste a bit of cayenne pepper, but not too much—enough to make little pricks on the roof of the mouth after the first few bites, but not enough to call the fire department.

Under the "flavoring" category on the ingredients label, Dot's Pretzels remains proprietarily mum, mentioning dried garlic and dried onion with an ambiguous "spices" thrown in to torment the inquirer.

Well, never mind. In the end, it's the balance and restraint of the ingredients that makes them so damn good, and so worth paying for. As we stand in the kitchen tasting them, Tom says, "I think this is the finest food ever made."

And others agree. Each year as I travel throughout the Midwest, I notice that Dot's Homestyle Pretzels are appearing in ever-widening circles in stores throughout Minnesota, South Dakota, Montana. (My sister Charlotte discovered them in Minneapolis and now recommends eating them with chocolate hummus.) They're all over now, and Dot's has spin-off products like pretzel-based candy bars with white and dark chocolate, pretzel crumbs, and a "pretzel rub" you can order from their website to put on chicken, pork, or fish.

Even Tom's brother who lives in Washington, DC, was talking about Dot's Homestyle Pretzels recently. "Those things are so addictive," he said when his daughter brought a bag home from college in Michigan, where Dot's Pretzels are now available.

When I finally found Dot's Homestyle Pretzels in the grocery store near my house in Ames, Iowa, I announced it with pride to the cashier—"these pretzels are from my home state!" (*OMG, have you tasted those?* she says. Like I didn't know.) It was something like the swell of pride I felt when the NDSU Bison came to Ames to beat up the Division I football team of the university where I teach, the Iowa State Cyclones—like my talented younger brother had come to town to defend my honor as an unrepentant North Dakotan.

And so you can travel the world and find yourself living elsewhere, but the tastes of home will haunt you. You can reach for it, but seldom attain it—not the taste itself and sometimes not even the memory of the taste. The Amish of eastern Iowa make rhubarb wine that tastes *almost* like Grandpa Geist's wine, but not quite. Amish pickled cucumbers and beets taste *almost* like Grandma's, but not exactly.

You can try to cook recipes from home, but they won't turn out tasting the same. You'll find that your Greek-American boyfriend wants to add garlic and olives to your knoephla soup. You'll find that later when you make your mother's caramel rolls for your stepsons, you double the cream-butter-brown-sugar quantities for the topping (in that extravagant way that is all your own) and they turn out to be jaw-droppingly good sticky buns of yumminess, but they are not your mother's caramel rolls. Not the ones that you and your sisters and brother devoured by the panful those afternoons when you got off the school bus.

And you'll be surprised to find that your grandma Marquart's kuchen recipe is proportioned to make an army-sized quantity of twenty-four kuchen and does not even bother to specify the measurement for flour—but just reads "flour," as if you should know. And so many of the cooks who knew how much flour are gone.

One of my colleagues who is Lebanese-American endeavored to follow his elderly great aunt around the kitchen to write down his favorite recipes exactly as she made them. She was getting old and she would not be around forever. He wanted his traditional dishes to taste exactly as she had made them. But when he was bending to write something down, he was surprised to discover through the corner of his eye that she was sneaking in little pinches of this and little drops of that into the pot. The taste of home can be furtive.

In what turned out to be the last time I saw my sister Judy, she was giving me a ride from our hometown, Napoleon, to the Bismarck Airport so that I could catch a flight home to Iowa. For the last few years, she had been working as a cook in the deli at the local grocery store, pushing out new creations and delectables that were expanding her renown as a caterer and knoephla sorceress.

That day, it worked out that she could give me a ride to the airport because her boss was sending her for some special culinary training at the regional headquarters of her store's food chain in Bismarck.

Over the years, no one had worked harder than my sister—holding down two jobs as the secretary at the high school during the day and managing the Korner Bar at night. But now she had settled into this job at the grocery store, and with the encouragement of her boss she was building up the deli section. She had reached a rightness, a new place of happiness in her work.

On the drive up from Napoleon, she bragged about how someone from Stan's Supermarket (of Wishek sausage fame) had been in touch with her about possibly supplying them with some of her homemade knoephla to sell in the store. It would require an investment to her home kitchen to make it professional grade, but she was pleased by the inquiry, the outside acknowledgment that she'd made something of quality that people wanted to buy.

She told me that the people from Stan's Supermarket had jokingly suggested to her, "Why don't you just give us the recipe?" and she'd fired right back with "Okay, I'll give you my knoephla recipe after you give me your recipe for Wishek sausage." I think the conversation ended right there.

Mrs. Schumacher Busts a Nut

We understood that Mrs. Schumacher's mind had once and for all slipped a gear that morning when we found the volleyball net cut into hundreds of little pieces. We'd forgotten ourselves the day before and left it hanging outside on the playground, swinging in a lazy dip between the two support poles.

"Drats," Randy Horner said. He bent low and ran his sunburnt fingers through the stringy pile. I knew it wasn't a swear word, but the sound of his voice, rough and too deep for an eighth-grader, always made my stomach do a little flip. He stood, shook his gold bangs out of his eyes and turned to face Mrs. Schumacher's house. Inside a cracked window, behind a faded drape, surely, there the old woman stood watching.

Later that morning Sister Paula spoke over the intercom about how we were a small school with an even smaller budget, and about how it was our own fault for not putting the volleyball net away. I imagined her in the principal's office—so small behind her very large desk, leaning into the microphone and pressing down the "on" button with her thumb.

"What this means in human terms," she said, and a groan ran through the school. Sister Paula always felt obliged to translate things to us in human terms, as if we were worms and germs with amoeba for brains.

"What this means," she whispered, keeping her voice even, "is that we will not be replacing it."

A sigh of protest raced through the school. From first grade to eighth, the high and low voices echoed along the wood floors, telegraphing through the walls, scratching their way onto the chalkboards.

We were bored, bored, bored at this school with no basketball games, no cheerleading squads, not even a team bus or a gymnasium. To think our parents actually paid money to send us to this school where early morning Mass was considered an outing. We were the good sheep, the eternally-found ones, the sisters reminded us daily, and the kids in the public school were the lost sheep. We should care more about the state of our souls, they warned, and less about the state of our playground.

Losing the volleyball net made everyone mad, but it especially made Randy Horner mad. He was the wildest boy in school, so wild that no one expected him to live past thirteen. He was most famous for his diving slides and suicidal saves. He'd stand up and raise the ball in his hand. Then he'd dust off his pantlegs, grab his crotch, and declare the save a "nut buster."

In volleyball, he liked to remind us, he was feared and revered for his overhand power serves. They were all unreturnable, but we came to separate them into two categories: palm sizzlers and knuckle crunchers.

It was Randy Horner, pretending to be a cowpoke in sixth grade, who commandeered a banana bike and lassoed Sally Bitz around the neck while she innocently guarded second base. It was he who stuffed a stocking cap into a hallway light fixture the winter before, starting a small electrical fire and causing school to be canceled for two days.

We all agreed Horner was the perfect name for Randy. When a thin layer of sweat appeared on his face, his forehead grew two prominent temple bumps that shone and, we swore, flexed like horns threatening to sprout. Every afternoon when he climbed the four steps of the southbound bus for the long ride home, a sigh of relief went through the crowd: Randy Horner had made it through another day.

In 1964, the year before Mrs. Schumacher busted a nut, the Bishop of the Diocese decided that the church of St. Philip—with its 50-foot fresco ceilings and gold-filigreed altar, and its statue of Jesus with his arms outstretched in a gesture of infinite compassion, and its statue of the Virgin Mary tenderly swaddling the Christ child in her arms while her dainty, sandaled foot crushed to utter flatness the evil slippery-tongued head of the serpent below—that this grand old church was to be demolished and replaced by a new, modern church.

The plans were elaborate. Neighboring houses would be bought up, parking lots expanded, the pipe organ replaced by an electric organ with a convenient overhead speaker system. "Exciting," the Bishop said in his letter to the parish, and there were those in town who were happy. But the oldest people in town, the immigrants who saw St. Philip Neri as a final vestige of their European childhoods, were not happy.

Early every morning, the widows hunched in black veils in their pews, working the hard beads of their rosaries, toiling in rows like so many women in a garment factory, producing a blanket of prayers to cover both the dead and the living. Their syllables were labored, heavy with grief—rough German echoing in the rafters.

Theirs had been lives of displacement, and now, at the end of long emigrations, they were ready for things to stay put. One hundred years before, their grandparents had moved from central Europe to the Russian empire seeking *Lebensraum*, and in their own lives they had fled Russia, coming to America seeking asylum.

Letters followed them from Russia, asking for food, telling of old women dying, whole villages disappearing. The old people felt helpless. They sent parcels to Russia, then were met with a new silence. St. Philip's became the place where they could go in the face of this numbing quiet, to light candles, to say prayers of remembrance and hope.

As the rafters of St. Philip's came down, the old people watched the workers from the Diocese carry away statues and chalices. It was then that they recalled again the Russia-letters, the stories of Bolsheviks looting churches and seizing grain. They recalled how steeples were knocked down, and the husk of the empty churches were used as storage bins and beer halls. Their memories were long like this, spread over centuries and continents, set on the hard things as they watched the tall rafters of St. Philip Neri fall.

The morning we found the volleyball net cut to ribbons, Randy Horner and some other boys from the eighth grade, set to work to put the thing back together. They scattered the pieces like a puzzle directly in front of Mrs. Schumacher's crowded picture window. They climbed around on their knees, yelling to each other about how they thought they had found a bit of edging here or a corner piece there.

Then Mrs. Schumacher came out of her house and went to work on her lawn. She had only a thin berm remaining between where the playground ended and her house began. To this small bit of grass, she took a hoe—her black dress blowing tight in the wind against her small frame.

Dunnerwetter, she screamed at the boys, her arms rising and falling in the air. The hollow maw of her face releasing the words we would never understand into the monstrous wind. The German-speaking kids translated for us. *Thunder weather*, they said, explaining it was a powerful curse coming from a woman who probably believed that God controlled all of nature and would use it against us, if she asked him to.

Gross hund, she muttered and pointed a knobby finger at Randy Horner. *You go back to the devil.*

Most of us laughed and hugged our sides. We jumped up and down at Mrs. Schumacher's rantings. But not Randy Horner. We didn't understand then about Randy—how his father was a widower who liked to drink too much and knock Randy around sometimes. How Randy understood the meaning of a curse. He stood up, leaving the crumbling volleyball net behind, and proceeded to bark words back at Mrs. Schumacher.

Schtinckscht, he yelled, making a show of holding his nose. He left the boys behind on the playground and moved toward her, speaking in those low tones, unearthly and guttural, that no one could translate. Mrs. Schumacher responded in high, bird-like squawks.

Nichts wisse, Mrs. Schumacher sang in a thin whine, as if answering his threats. Leaning on her hoe, she shook her finger back and forth at Randy Horner to shame him—*know nothing, know nothing*.

This seemed to make him more mad. He met Mrs. Schumacher on the edge of her hacked-up lawn—his head thrown back, his chest inflated. He moved closer, careful to stay out of range of her suspended hoe. He mumbled and repeated words too quiet for anyone to hear.

He stopped a few feet shy of where Mrs. Schumacher hung on the edge of her tattered berm. He looked at her with the coldest stare, the ice-blue eyes that we now, from watching too much television, have come to associate with mass murderers and Nazi commandants.

Mrs. Schumacher locked her watery blue eyes against the hardness of his eyes. She seemed planted there that day, like a tree with a hard wind at her back, as if a force greater than her own will kept her there.

The new building that rose out of the ruins of St. Philip Neri was a wonder of steel and glass. Round and low to the ground, it looked like a flying saucer rotating on its base.

After the strange church finally ceased to spin, a brand-new priest stepped out of the saucer church. Transferred to some unknown location, was their old priest Father Veit, who had been there for twenty-five years, separating the chaff of petty venials from the hard kernel of mortal sins. He had doled out penance and promised forgiveness, performing *extreme unction* at deathbeds, and guaranteeing the soul's safe passage. But he was best loved for his ability to fudge the eulogy so effectively as to make even the most rotten individual sound worthy.

Now his replacement was Father Kroeller. He was no younger than Father Veit, but he seemed to be made of some indestructible material. He had a powerful jaw and a handshake to match. Some people had heard of him before and said he was known in the Diocese as the Building Priest. He spoke broken English with a high-German accent, not the enclaved low-German that the people of the town spoke, which signaled to them that he was a real German, recently emigrated from Germany. This caused them to instantly distrust him.

He had a shock of white hair standing up as if at constant attention on the top of his head. He walked with a sideways gait, and a vigorous limp, crooking his head to the left when he spoke. When it was rumored that he had been shot in the neck during

World War II, the people could only speculate they were harboring a Nazi fugitive, possibly an SS man.

Father Kroeller was what my father called a mover and a shaker. He worked the crowd like a politician, shaking hands, nodding his head and smiling as if he were listening attentively, but the old people suspected he had no idea who they were or what their family names meant.

At the parish meetings, he enthusiastically unfolded a blueprint with all the improvements the Diocese envisioned. In the plan, the new church and parochial school were to be joined into a modern complex, and to that a new parsonage would be added. The priest's new house would have a wide, stone chimney, a vaulted ceiling, plush carpets, a large dining room, a massive study, plenty of bedrooms, and an ample kitchen, deep in the heart of the house.

The sight of such splendor caused people to wonder about the oath of poverty. The only other house in town that was larger than the plan for Father Kroeller's belonged to the Wentz family, and they didn't count because they owned the town café and the car dealership. The house was so large that it would require a live-in maid—Father Kroeller's sister Ina recently emigrated from Germany. For a small fee, she would also cook.

"One never knows when the Bishop might choose to visit," Father Kroeller was reported to have said.

The blueprint unfurled further and released the plans hidden in its deepest folds. The old houses close to the church would be bought up, and the old people in them would be relocated—everything in the vicinity leveled and asphalted into neat yellow diagonals for parking spaces. Looking at it from above, the neat blue lines of the Bishop's plan were a beautiful sight to behold.

But there was one snag, and that was Mrs. Schumacher. She lived behind the parochial school and may have been the only person whose name Father Kroeller took the time to remember, because he needed her cooperation. He visited her several times a week, standing on her sidewalk, talking as she whisked the dirt from her concrete steps.

He said, "These are fine hollyhocks, Frau Schumacher." He said, "May I trouble you for some delicious tomatoes from your garden?"

Father Kroeller spent hours like this outside of Mrs. Schumacher's house, rambling on about the Diocese and the plans. How the church was willing to pay good money for this little plot of land on which her old clapboard house and trembling pigeon barn barely stood.

The land was not for sale, no, and what would become of her perennials? Her children were born in that house, and her husband had died there. And who was he to ask for tomatoes from her garden? She wasn't dead yet, and she planned to eat them all herself. These were the things we listened to Mrs. Schumacher grumble about during recess as she worked in the garden.

The result of her stubbornness was that, when the project was complete, Mrs. Schumacher's house appeared to float like an island of weeds and garbage, loose boards and cracked windows directly in the center of the smooth ocean of the church parking lot. The house reminded me sometimes of a barge that had been lost at sea for a long time—the clothing hanging on the line like sails, growing more and more ragged as time passed, becoming less and less able to catch the necessary wind that would return its passenger to civilization.

The day after she cut the volleyball net to ribbons, Mrs. Schumacher began to patrol her borders, running the perimeter like a rabid dog, barking in German if we came too close. We knotted the volleyball net back together and resumed play. A couple times the ball went wild and strayed onto her property, and then we just had to consider it gone. We lost three balls that way in a matter of weeks, having watched each one roll innocently into her slim grove of trees.

The only time Mrs. Schumacher left her property was on Tuesday mornings when her son Bud, a fifty-year-old bachelor, picked her up in his blue Chevy and took her grocery shopping. He'd run his right tire straight into the crack between the tiny berm and the asphalt, precisely where it had been chopped off by the church. Then he pulled the emergency brake and honked his horn, sitting in the car toking on a cigarette while he waited for his mother.

She came out of her front door, a shawl wrapped around her thinning white hair. Her walk was bow-legged and determined, making her way to Bud's car with a purse slung savagely across her forearm. She opened the door and stepped wide into Bud's Chevy—careful to avoid the asphalt, as if she couldn't bear to set foot on anything belonging to the Catholic Church.

We observed this every Tuesday morning from our classroom while Sister Jacinta rattled on about the Battle of Little Bighorn or the Trail of Tears or whatever epoch in American history she felt compelled to teach us that day. *What is history but a fable agreed-upon*, Napoleon said. And even though I knew Mrs. Schumacher and was there when it happened, the events remain foggy to me.

Maybe it's like the time my sister saw a flying saucer. It was winter. We were sitting in the living room watching *Bonanza* with our buttery popcorn bowls when all of a sudden, my sister jumps up, her popcorn flying in all directions.

"A flying saucer," she screams. She races to the picture window. "A flying saucer."

"What?" We all put down our bowls. In seconds we're gathered at the window—my mother from her sewing room, my brother from his bedroom upstairs. "What did you see?" we say. "What?"

"A flying saucer," my sister repeats. She's so excited the spit is flying from her mouth. "It dipped right down. There in front of the garage," she says, making wide zooming motions with her arms. "And then it went up."

"Nonsense," we all say, "there's no such thing as a flying saucer."

"I saw it," she screams, her eyes getting more wild. "It was silver and round," she says, adding details. "It had blue rotating lights in a circle around the bottom. It dipped right down and then it was gone."

She went on and on like this, her hand motions becoming less and less dramatic as we went back to our seats and took back up our bowls of popcorn. Soon she was the only one by the window, holding onto the edge of the sill, repeating that hard kernel, insisting on the story, which none of us believed.

On the day Mrs. Schumacher busted a nut, as soon as she pulled out of the parking lot in Bud's blue Chevy, Randy Horner raised his hand and asked if he could be excused to the bathroom. A few minutes later, I saw him step into the sunlight of the parking lot. He moved quickly toward Mrs. Schumacher's house, hunching low to the ground like a combat soldier. Over his right shoulder, a small hunting rifle was slung. It looked no bigger than the gun my brother used to hunt gophers on Saturday afternoons. I was used to guns, but still I was surprised to see one, here at school.

When he got to Mrs. Schumacher's property, he stepped onto her lawn, easing his foot a bit, like he was boarding a raft and thought the thing might give way underneath him. He dropped to a crouch and spider-crawled across the lawn, disappearing into the cluster of trees beside Mrs. Schumacher's sagging barn. We watched all this as Sister Jacinta rattled on about Custer's Last Stand.

A few minutes later, the three volleyballs rolled out one at time. Then Randy Horner followed, his pockets seemingly stuffed with a lifetime of lost baseballs. The rifle was back on his shoulder, and in his hands he gripped the outstretched claws of dead pigeons, their speckled wings collapsing and falling wide under the pull of gravity.

We watched as Randy Horner dropped a pigeon, squat, on Mrs. Schumacher's front step. We watched as he made his way across the parking lot, dropping pigeons at perfectly even intervals, like a trail he was leaving for someone he was afraid might get lost.

This is what it looked like thirty minutes later when Bud's Chevy pulled into the driveway, full of Mrs. Schumacher and all her groceries. The old woman flew from the car like a woman of twenty. She moved so fast it was stunning and unnatural. She was like that old woman who finds her way to your dreams, who can always fly faster than you can run, because you can't run at all because your muscles are slogging through wet cement. And always when she's almost overtaken you, just nipping your ankles, that's when you wake up in the middle of the dark night. That's how quickly Mrs. Schumacher flew that day.

She bent to the ground, gathering pigeons to her chest, collecting them in her arms, each pigeon bringing her closer and closer to the school, as her son Bud followed her, a cigarette hanging from his lip, bending as she bent, begging her to, *please*, Mother, *please*, come in the house.

This was appearing to us through the classroom window, you understand, like a film we were watching, like something under glass—Bud finally grabbing his mother's arm and dragging her across the parking lot, pulling her up her steps and into her crumbling house.

Everything took on a dreamy quality for the rest of the day, like a movie we weren't allowed to go to. But during our noon-hour recess, she appeared on the playground again, this time carrying a fat, glistening butcher knife.

She moved across the sidewalk like a sleeper, walking a line straight to the center of the crowd where Randy Horner stood, horsing around with a group of boys who spread wide in a half-circle away from Randy Horner. He stood in the center, not surprised to see her, with his hands out in a cool way as if to say, *C'mon.*

What I remember next is the high-pitched screams of the smaller kids and the folds of the sisters' heavy cloaks as they collected us in groups. I never saw what happened, so here's what those who say they saw it said.

She never hacked away at him, like you would have expected. They say she just held that knife steady at an angle, pointed at him, as if the knife were now attached to her hand—like it would never be a knife again, and her hand never just a hand.

In the background was the screaming of children and the flapping of cloaks that sounded like so many birds taking off. We were herded into the school, each sister taking a group into a classroom and bolting the door. I got stuck in the library with Sister Thomasina, a bunch of books, and a row of windows that faced the street away from the playground.

The people who say they saw what happened, claim that Mrs. Schumacher went right through him, like a car cutting through fog. For weeks after that, we argued about it. Some people said that Mrs. Schumacher was dead and that was her big-ghost self, carrying a big-ghost knife, which she would now be destined to carry around for the rest of eternity.

Some people said that Randy Horner just fell, or slipped, or dodged her, but I never believed that story. Randy Horner had balance like you wouldn't believe, and he never backed away from anything in his life. None of us ever saw Mrs. Schumacher again, so maybe that's some kind of proof.

Maybe it's like the way my father found circles in the snow the morning after my sister saw the flying saucer. When he went out to do the chores, he found three identical circles, all the same width and depth—one behind the barn, one in the backyard, and one in front of the picture window where my sister said the saucer had set down for a moment.

We all went outside to look at them. My sister following us from circle to circle, planting herself on the perimeter telling us again what she had seen. We retreated to the house in a tight pack, mulling it over silently.

We didn't take photographs. At the time it seemed stupid to take pictures of snow. A few days later when it heated up, everything melted, and the circles disappeared.

Sometimes even now when we get together, we argue about it. There are those who say nothing happened—that there were no blue lights, that there were no circles in the snow. They cling to that belief, standing firmly on the edge of it, and they will not, for anything, be moved.

The Art of the Cheer

Poetry was no longer a strange and irrelevant loveliness in a chaotic world; it was a necessary and consummate flowering on the great tree of life; it was the immanent purpose of the universe made vocal.

— Elizabeth Sewell, *The Orphic Voice*

1.

The afternoon I bought my first record, *Red Rubber Ball*, by the Cyrkle, I went to my best friend Jovita's house. She plucked the single from the sleeve and dropped it onto her turntable with a crunch of the needle as the sound of the Farfisa organ rang out, and we danced the Pony on the bouncy, wood floor of her upstairs bedroom. I went to her house often, late afternoons, after Catholic school, while her parents were still at work at their grocery store.

It was the first metaphor I understood to be a metaphor (*The rollercoaster ride we took is nearly at an end*) and perhaps the first simile (*The morning sun is rising like a red rubber ball*), because we talked about such things, the poetry of song lyrics, just as we wore each other's clothes and secretly applied her older sister's make-up on each other's eyes and cheeks and lips, trying out our future faces.

2.

And in Jovita's bedroom, where we went to get away from her four pesky younger brothers, we made up moves and cheers to accompany pivotal moments in imaginary games to come: *Push 'em* **back***, push 'em* **back***, push 'em* **waay back** and *Let's go, let's go, L-E-T-S-G-O.* Our hands clapping, our feet stomping as we released our cheers, our vowels and consonants like desire into the world.

And she was always better at it than me, getting the body's motions to mirror the meaning of the words, all of which she made up, and which I learned from her and mimicked so that the cheer's effect would be doubled in the world.

This was 1966, years before Title IX would reach us. We were tiny beings anyway, ten-year-old girls, our skinny bodies preparing to take our place on the sidelines, preparing to raise our voices in meaningful, structured ways, all in an attempt to embolden the giants among us.

3.

The game of basketball is a closed and finite experiment designed to test the mettle and training, the natural talents and improvisational skills of its participants. The confines of the game's structure create the effect of heightened drama, because, unlike life, every moment of a basketball game reminds us that something is at stake.

The game unfolds with cold precision, in pre-set increments of time, the passage of which ticks away in minutes and seconds on a wall display, and whose expiration is announced by horns and buzzers. In basketball, there can be no mystery about where the time has gone; yet, it often slips away inexplicably.

The playing court, too, is defined and pre-set, a long rectangle of dark floor marks indicating in-bounds, out-of-bounds, front and back court, the free-throw line, the ten-second line, the top of the key—all agreed-upon spaces in which certain things may or may not occur, but places in which invariably many wrong and unfortunate things do occur. Referees dressed in black-and-white-striped shirts, to differentiate them from the players, are present on the floor among the players with their whistles to point out, monitor, and officiate the infractions.

The game's impeccable intentions stand in high relief to the foibles of humans, the fumbling inaccuracies, the missteps and double dribbles, the winded back-and-forth rushes of sweaty bodies, the wild passes.

In this small interpretative space, where time slips away, where rules are broken and penalties are incurred, a few humans manage to structure moments that coordinate the mastery of eye and hand, breath and foot that makes basketball unfold like poetry. And it is here, I would suggest, where cheers artfully enough designed might also enter the game's calculus and influence outcomes in infinitesimal ways.

4.

My ex-husband told me about the years when he was a young boy, praying in his upstairs bedroom in Rapid City, South Dakota, praying in the bathroom on the toilet, praying in the shower, praying before he went to bed, for the St. Louis Hawks, the Minnesota Lakers, the Philadelphia 76ers, praying for anyone to beat the Celtics.

Then one day he had this thought—was some other boy, possibly in New England, praying more fervently in the bathroom on the toilet, in the shower, praying in bed each day of each year, for the Celtics to win? And weren't there more of such boys in New England than the unpopulated West? So he wondered, do the prayers of opposing fans cancel each other out and does one team prosper in the imbalance?

Which caused him to puzzle out if God had a team, and, if so, was he Catholic? Or did God watch over the conflagrations of humans like a dispassionate Zeus, while Athena, Apollo and Artemis interfered with the outcomes of our mortal play?

5.

When it comes up, because it always seems to come up, what we did back in high school, I'll admit I was a cheerleader. In a small town, everyone has to be at least five things—school newspaper, choir, 4-H, drama club, cheerleader—in order for the town to function like a proper town. It could have been worse. Braddock, a smaller town thirty miles away, had only one boy in a senior class with eight girls. Imagine how stressful homecoming was for him. Imagine his prom.

We were growing up in Napoleon, North Dakota, a town of short fierce people named after a short, fierce emperor. At five foot, four inches, I was a female giant in my tribe. Sometimes, at family gatherings, the grandparents would point at me with pride and say, "Look at her long legs."

We were the Imperials, rolling from town to town in my uncle Ben's school bus in our royal blue and white uniforms. With our short limbs and low centers of gravity, we were born grapplers (North Dakota Class B High School Wrestling Champions: 1975, 1980, 1981, 1982, 1989, 1990, 1997, 2002, 2003, 2004, 2005, 2006, 2007). Yet, I chose to try out for the basketball cheering squad, which reveals my natural instinct to root for the underdog and prefigures my lifelong weakness for the Vikings and the Knicks.

6.

Into the taut spatial and temporal construct of a basketball game, adversaries must step with only this one round ball to share and fight over among ten players, five people per team. Off the court, they may be friends or admirers, lovers or co-workers, sisters or brothers, but here on the court, everything becomes

Either-Or—teammate or opponent, offense or defense—switching back and forth throughout the game in infinite varieties and configurations.

Above all this, suspended at a lofty height is the game's other plane, the backboards, the orange rims, and the empty floating nets of the two baskets at either end, to be scored upon or defended. Two empty nets, but only one ball.

The purity of their emptiness drives the action, causing players to pass, to run, to block, to steal, to fumble, to foul, all driven by the urge to fill the opponent's void with the ball in your possession, however momentarily, to feel the swish that will result in a score that will finally count for something.

7.

Those afternoons at Jovita's house, before we were old enough to be cheerleaders, we practiced the high jump, the splits, the hand motions, the sequence of hand claps. We mastered the cartwheel, the back and front flips. We became athletes of cheering.

Our first utterances, the sounds we made in grade school—whispers behind cupped hands, gum pops, sighs, gasps, laughs—grew more organized and filled with intention as we matured. Our sounds made their way to talk, to chatter, to songs, which made their way to bad rhymes, then bad poems written in wide-ruled notebooks in sprawls of pink and green ink about bad boys, about boys who didn't notice, about boys who had the moves. *Ronnie, Ronnie, he's our man. If he can't do it, no one can.*

At last, finally, we were selected, given license, to yell, to jump, to scream along the sidelines. We were put in charge of pep; we were given a rally. People got out of fifth period and were required to file onto the bleachers and listen to us as we jumped and shouted about the importance of pep until the whole student body learned the cheers along with us, so that we could organize their shouting when the critical moment arrived, so that the effect would be multiplied again and again.

The pep rally had its own highs and lows, sobering moments when an injured hero was acknowledged, when the direness of the situation was explained by the coaches. Then the team was called out to the gymnasium floor in their sports coats and ties, where we led a cheer for them, attempting to fill up our team, contaminate them with pep, so that we could send them into battle brimming with encouragement.

During the chaos of the games, it was our job to transform the untrained and random sounds of the crowd—the frustrated voices shouting *C'mon* or *Airball* or *Good Job*—and harness them inside the amplified crucible of the gym into **De-fense, De-fense, stomp**-*stomp*, **stomp**-*stomp-stomp*, so that the words would break through and rearrange the heartbeats of our champions.

8.

The acoustic landscape of a basketball game is full of noise and cheers, wishes and curses. It's full of prayers, chants, and incantations, coming from all parties and moving in all directions. Fans scream and call and plead their way into the game. Athletes pray, and trash talk, and wish, and curse—at each other, at the refs, into the ethers, into the heavens, calling on reserves, calling on favors.

Does this ur-language make a space where something happens? Before poems and prayers, there were spells and charms—carefully arranged words selected not only for their figurative and literal meanings, but also for their acoustic value, arranged and vocalized in specific, ritualized ways so that they would travel through the waves of the world and effect change on the material plane.

9.

I'll admit I've imagined a world where poets would fill stadiums as athletes and rock stars now do. Where droves of people would fight traffic, take time off from work, to stand in line and rush to buy merchandise that's far too expensive—tickets, t-shirts, beer, hotdogs—all the while wishing they could get back to their seats where they could scream and chant and cheer over a well-turned phrase, over the beauty of an image, the ingenuity of a metaphor.

I've imagined people so enraptured with poetry performances that they would recondition their RVs and show up early at stadiums, tailgating in cold parking lots, drinking beer and grilling burgers with total strangers, just so they could prolong the anticipation and the experience of hearing poetry read. Crazy talk, I know. But what is basketball but ten men in shorts, two empty baskets, and their desire to fill it with the one ball allowed in the game?

Imagine: *A poem is a closed and finite experiment designed to test the mettle and training, the natural talents and improvisational skills of its participants. The confines of the poem's structure create the effect of heightened drama, because, unlike life, every moment of a poem reminds us that something is at stake.*

10.

"Poetry makes nothing happen," Auden wrote. But what is the *nothing* about which Auden speaks? Does he simply mean that poetry doesn't fix potholes? That the world is made by the doers and that poetry has no effect or value in the material world?

Or when he speaks of the *nothing* that poetry makes happen, does he mean the expression of the rare and intangible thing, the ineffable, which is all around us but difficult to communicate because of its scale, especially with such small instruments as words and actions—like teaspoons measuring oceans. Most days, the magnitude registers as a void. Perhaps this is why prophets go to the desert, why tourists go to the Grand Canyon.

Sometimes, if the world goes silent for a moment, we might cognize a small increment that intimates the largeness, but when we attempt to speak of it, the very sounding makes the ineffable move out of view. The words remain for us to use to remind us of the larger things that stand behind them in silence.

I've felt this absence of presence in rare moments after I've given a poetry reading or taught a class, when I prepare to leave the room, but look around one last time because I feel as if I've forgotten something there.

I've felt this presence, alone in the gym, after a long night of cheering, after things were decided and the game was won or lost—in the humming glare of the fluorescent lights, the gloss of the wax floor, the lingering smell of popcorn.

And I've observed it in the chaos of competition, in moments of near perfection that arrive with such elegance—the high diver's body entering the pool without a splash; the inaudible swish of the perfect jump shot.

Surely this is approaching the ineffable—to enter the water without the water knowing it, to put the ball through the hoop without troubling the net. It gives one hope. And surely this is what poets try for every day, arranging acoustic elegances that will intimate the magnitude. Surely this is what all the fuss—all the cheering, the crying and gnashing of teeth—is ultimately about.

The Night We Landed on the Moon

The summer my friend Susan's sister got pregnant and had to be sent away was the summer we landed on the moon. The night we landed on the moon, Susan and I were walking down the sidewalk to my grandmother's house. Susan was explaining to me how it was that Audrey had gotten pregnant. I was concerned about Audrey having to move away, mostly because what little I knew about sex, I had learned from her through Susan, and I feared the interruption of my sex education.

"The guy has a thing," Susan says. "And it gets big, and he sticks it in you and it shoots this stuff in there that smells like Hi-lex."

"No way," I say and slug her in the arm.

"Yes way," she says and slugs me back. I'm busy trying to figure out the logistics of this, like exactly which parts of the body are involved. During study hall, Susan would straighten the barrette in her silky golden hair, cup her hand to the side of her mouth and proceed to tell me that Tussy was the only deodorant to use, not Right Guard, like the older girls used in gym class. And if you wore perfume, it should be Musk and you should put it in certain places on your body—the insides of your thighs, in between your boobs, on your throat, and, of course, on the insides of your wrists. Her sister Audrey had told Susan these were the places a boy was sure to go.

Audrey was once flat-chested, Susan told me, just like us and now she had huge boobs. She'd seen Audrey's naked boobs in the bathtub one evening, so she assured me that our boobs would be that way someday. I had never seen my sisters' naked boobs, so I assumed that boobs ran only in Susan's family.

Earlier that year, the nuns had instructed all the farmgirls and all the towngirls about the monthly blessing that nature gives all women. Should nuns be entrusted with the sex education of young girls?

The sisters shepherded us into a classroom during recess. They drew the curtains and pulled the door shades. They covered up the skylights. We all sat very quietly in the darkness, the towngirls and the farmgirls alike, waiting to find out what we had done wrong. Then Sister Jacinta burst through the door with a movie projector on a cart. On the lower shelf was a neat stack of pamphlets. The movie, the projector, the cart, and the pamphlets were all the same antiseptic shade of mint green.

The sisters handed the pamphlets out, one to each girl. I remember the smooth newness of the pamphlet in my hands. The light green cover was splashed with white asterisks that looked like the jacks from the game ball and jacks.

I thumbed through the pamphlet by the light of the projector. It had illustrations of a girl my age going through several phases of realization. On every page there was a light bulb going on over the girl's head. On the last page, she smiled knowingly.

The film was not a film at all, but a slide show with a scratchy record playing in the background. The record would beep, and Sister Jacinta would advance to the next frame. The record droned on and on. I started to hear the boys coming back from recess— the farmboys and the townboys. I could hear them in the hallway, laughing and slamming their lockers. I could see their pantlegs shadowing the slats at the bottom of the door as they tried to peer into the classroom.

I knew I would die if they caught me watching this movie. I knew I would die if they found out what we were just now being told. I knew that when we got out of the room, Stevie Schnable would try to pinch and twist my boobs until I told him everything that we had been shown. I slipped the pamphlet deep in my bookbag and decided I would read it when I got home.

All the way home that day on the bus, I thought about that cool green pamphlet in my bookbag, and how I was going to bring it out into the light of day and read it when I got to my bedroom.

That afternoon when I got home, my mother was sewing in the utility room. The fabric she was working on was draped all over her lap and on the floor like a shroud. I waited beside the ironing board while my sisters and brother went past. My mother looked up at me with pins sticking out of her mouth.

"That's nice material," I said. "What are you making?"

"Curtains," she said through the pins, "for your brother's room."

I opened the clasp of my bookbag and dug deep for the pamphlet. I laid it on the ironing board and leaned over the edge of the sewing table. "We learned about this in school today," I whispered. "The sisters showed us a movie."

My mother picked up the pamphlet. She got a funny look on her face, the kind my brother got when I caught him in the middle of a lie—a little embarrassed, a little guilty, maybe a little surprised. She glanced at the book with the white asterisks that looked like jacks from the game ball and jacks, then she said, "You won't need to know about this for a while."

She slid the book into the folds of fabric beside her sewing machine. She always kept her extra fabric on the table to the right of her machine. She might keep a piece of material there for years until she found just the right pattern, then she'd work feverishly, staying up half the night, fitting the pattern to the material, cutting it into pieces and then sewing it together into some useful, new shape.

My mother stored stacks and stacks of material there for years on end. Later that day, I went back to search for the mint green pamphlet in the folds of my mother's fabric, but I couldn't find it. I never saw the book again.

That night, the night we landed on the moon, when Susan and I were walking down the sidewalk to my grandma's house, and Susan was telling me about how her sister Audrey had gotten pregnant and had to move away, there was a carnival in town.

My grandma lived on the long main street with a U-turn on the end. Sometimes I'd sit on her porch and watch people drive by and then, a few minutes later, drive by again. I'd waved to them both times. Across from her house was the city park and sometimes on Sundays after church we would have dinner at her house and then go to swing and slide.

But the night we landed on the moon, the whole street was barricaded off, from uptown all the way to the U-turn because of the carnival. The Ferris wheel was set up right outside Grandma's front steps, and Susan and I sat on the porch watching people climb on and off the big rotating wheel. They screamed and rocked as their creaky seats went around and around. When they got stuck on top, we looked up and all we could see was the worn-out bottoms of their shoes.

It was the middle of July. A hot and humid night and Grandma had all her windows open. Inside we could hear the TV. Grandpa was the kind who could watch TV for hours without moving. He'd sit up straight on the couch, his hands folded over his stomach and watch. No talk of cards or attempts at conversation would distract him.

"For heaven's sake," I heard my grandma say. "Come and look at this." I went into the living room and there on the black and white screen was the pockmarked surface of the moon. An astronaut in a puffy white suit with hoses attached bounced as he walked. He carried an American flag, which he finally poked into the ground. "Isn't that something?" my grandma said.

Grandpa watched the screen. He did not blink.

I loved staying at Grandma's house because she always made me Tang in the mornings, the drink of astronauts. When I'd get up, she'd stir me a glass. She and Grandpa ate breakfast early because, although they moved in from the farm years before, they were still country people and they still got up at five o'clock. But they let me sleep as late as I pleased, and when I got up they made me an egg and Tang.

As I ate, she'd sit across the table from me, and we'd listen to a religious talk show on the radio. There were callers with soul-searching questions to which the minister responded. Sometimes they'd have interviews, and sometimes they'd read letters from fans. Eventually there were hymns. This was my grandma's favorite part; she'd hum along. She was a very religious woman, I thought, for a Lutheran.

I'd have lived with her forever if my parents would let me. When I stayed there, I had my own room, and at night I'd lie on the clean, hard surface of her guest-room bed and listen to the grandfather clock in the living room. I'd fall asleep making up songs and stories to go along with the ticking of the clock.

That night, the night we landed on the moon, after we watched the moon landing on TV, my grandpa surprised everyone by getting off the couch and going out to the porch. He looked up in the sky for the moon, but it was low on the horizon and the Ferris wheel was covering it. He stood out there for about half an hour, just staring at the moon where it would have been if the Ferris wheel had not been covering it, then he went inside to watch the news.

I sat with my grandmother on the porch and watched people walk up and down the midway looking for lost family members. *Have you seen so-and-so? Well if you do, tell them we're going.* Children were crying because they didn't want to go home, and parents were saying things like *If you keep acting like this, I'm never taking you anywhere again.*

Grandma pointed to the moon with a heavy arm and said, "Tell your grandpa that he can see the moon now if he wants."

"Grandpa," I called through the screen. "The moon is up."

"Imagine that," she said, "those men. All the way up there." We sat in silence for a long time, staring at the moon. She sighed. "Think of their poor wives."

"Grandma," I finally said. "When you were young, did something really bad happen to you?"

"Sure," she said, in her sad way. "Lots of bad things happened. I lost my mom. I had to raise all my brothers and sisters."

"No, I mean something different."

"Like what?" she asked.

"Like bleeding," I said, looking her square in the face.

"Did that happen to you?" she asked.

"No," I said, "but I heard about it."

She turned to face me. "Sure, I remember when it happened to me," she said. "I never liked my stepmother. When I started to bleed, I thought I was dying. I didn't want her to know, so I got old rags and stuffed them down there. Then I burned them at night so that no one would know."

"Were you dying?" I asked.

"No. It went away in a few days. I was so happy. I thought, oh, I got lucky and everything inside healed. But it came back again later."

We sat and looked at the street for a long time. The music had quieted down and the carnies were tearing apart the rides. They moved slowly in the streetlight.

I tried to find a way to describe to my grandmother this heaviness I was feeling, as if every cell in my body had taken on some new kind of gravity. We sat together on her porch and watched the carnies move slowly in the dim light with their wrenches and hammers. The organ music was replaced by the clanking of machinery being dismantled. There was swearing and occasionally, far off, you could hear a woman laugh. All the rides I had just been on lay in heaps up and down the length of the U-turn street.

The boy who ran the Ferris wheel bent over in front of me to pick up a large bundle of steel. He looked young, only a few years older than me. He had taken off his shirt and his tanned skin was shiny from sweat. His back was broad and fanned out at his shoulders like a picture I'd seen in the encyclopedia of a cobra getting ready to strike.

Two other carnies were giving him a hard time, calling him a pussy. They were tired, they said, of the way he was always sloughing off. They pointed to me and said that I could probably lift more than he could. They asked me, "Hey there, girl, do you want to join the carnival?"

He looked up at me and smiled. I watched him, the way his dark hair draped down the back of his neck as he carried the bundle of steel girders to a trailer at the far end of the street. As he turned and walked toward me in the streetlight, the angles of his face and chest reminded me of the moon, the way it looked on TV, with its flat surfaces and light, and its deep shadowed crevices.

When he bent again in front of me to pick up another bundle, I noticed he was wearing boots, and I liked the way that I could not see his ankles when his pantlegs pulled up. I vowed to never love a man who exposed his ankles in public. All I wanted to see was the wideness of his palms, the thinness of his waist, the narrowness of his hips.

II.

They live there because they have always lived there, because they were born there, and because to leave would be to have their hearts broken when they return. For they would find it gone. But there, and between the two—a chasm that absorbs everything.

—Melissa Holbrook Pierson, *The Place You Love is Gone*

At 79, My Mother Decides
to Plant Trees

*A society grows great when old men plant trees in whose
shade they can never hope to sit.*

—Greek Proverb

They loom over us like sequoias, our parents. In my first holy
communion photos, they flank me, grave and unsmiling in formal black clothes—my father's wool suit, my mother's boucle
skirt, long gloves, and short jacket. Her lips a bright smear of
red. Nuns surround me in the other photos—Sister Jacinta, Sister
Paula, my prison guards—their white coifs pulled tight around
foreheads, dark tunics heavy and flowing to the floor, drawn tight
at the waist by rosary beads.

I am the sapling between them in a white dress, white tights,
shoes, and a lace veil with a chaplet of flowers crowning my head.
My face looks thin and drawn, stricken even. Dark circles under
my eyes, the celebrant not celebrating. Have I drunk too deeply of
the communion wine? No, by this age I have sampled Grandpa's
rhubarb wine and wedding whiskey. I know the swirl.

Have I misunderstood the lessons of transubstantiation, taken too seriously the metaphor of eating the body of Christ? I hate meat. Our dairy cows and their calves are my friends, as are the dogs, cats, and chickens. Sitting too long at the kitchen table has become my nightly ritual, moving steak around on the plate, obscuring it under mashed potatoes and green beans. My mother's despairing calls from the kitchen that I am too frail. My father yelling from the living room, already watching his favorite show. *She'll eat when she's hungry.*

They were not giants outside of time, I will learn later—my father, barely five-foot-six; my mother, five-two. Sister Paula, our principal, just under five feet. The little generals of my childhood. By the time of this photo, they've baptized me unwittingly, initiated me into confession and penance, and now brought me through communion. They've broken the bad news in increments.

Second grade, and even the pope agrees, I have reached the age of reason. I am coming to realize the snare of mortality—to be born into life without consent and with no good alternative for how to exit. None of this is reasonable.

They are all gone now, except my mother, eroded off the edge of a disappearing hillside. The nuns to nun-retirement and nun-nursing-homes where we would learn, one-by-one, the news of their deaths. No one, not even Jesus to save them.

And my father, gone off the edge of a cliff, never to be heard from again. Goodbye, goodbye. Despite the dirty trick you played on me. Thank you. I love you.

I have a friend who says, *times change; people do not.* But that hasn't been my observation. Take my mother, for example—aside from a brief splash of turquoise on her kitchen walls in 1966, my mother remained faithful to taupe and green: olive side chairs, mossy drapes, avocado shag. Then at seventy, she visited my sister in Montana and came home in mad love with the color pink. And not just pastel pink, but hot fuchsia, throbbing magenta.

What happened? During the trip, my sister's friend Jennifer gave my mother a pair of hot pink sneakers with hand-appliqued sparkles. And that was enough. She was pinked. Once home, she painted her bedroom walls a shade somewhere between bubble-gum and polka-dot pink, requiring new pink sheets, comforters, and pajamas.

Who knew change could be so easy? After that, pink earrings, sweaters, and scarves followed. My father had died a few years earlier, and it seems for the first time in her adult life my mother had time to consider what colors she preferred.

This was all good news. Because what can you possibly buy to entertain and delight your seventy-year-old mother each year for Christmas, birthdays, and Mother's Day? How many crystal-line angels, La-Z-Boy recliners, and yearly subscriptions to Net-flix docs one mother need? She once begged me to stop buying her coffee makers. Three years in a row I sent her single-brew systems because she'd once murmured the slightest interest un-der her breath while watching a Keurig commercial (*Well, that's interesting*). And she doesn't even *like* coffee.

So now it's pink necklaces and handbags, pink bath towels, and shoes with more pink glittery hand-appliqued stars on them. One year, we siblings went together on a pink PT Cruiser step-through bike with whitewall tires, a little bell, and a pink woven basket mounted on the handlebars. I doubt she's ever dared to ride it around the block for fear of falling and breaking a hip, but still, it was pink!

Maybe it's just Montana, because at age seventy-nine, once again my mother went to Bozeman to visit my oldest sister (on the Greyhound this time because she now refuses to fly) and while there she goes to dinner at the home of Jennifer and Jack. That Jennifer—what is it about her? She's a master landscaper. Af-ter dinner, they sit in the backyard in the shadow of Bridger Bowl, under the canopy of Jennifer's trees listening to cicadas as the light goes down. And perhaps under the influence of some sweet pink wine, my mother develops this intense craving for trees.

How could she have lived all these years without the cool swaying of trees?

She and my dad moved from the farm to the brand-new house on a corner lot in town, kitty-corner from the Catholic church in 1981 and it has not occurred to her before this moment how much she misses her trees: the tall cottonwoods, the orchard rows that Great-Grandpa planted, the chokecherries, the conifers we watered as kids.

Then and there, she makes up her mind—she needs to go home and plant some trees!

Which is not as easy as you might imagine. She tells me all this when I call to catch up. Not weekly, sometimes barely monthly. Although we both have phone plans with unlimited minutes, we still practice the 1960s protocol of not making a long-distance call unless the barn burns down or someone gets decapitated in an automobile accident. Because, *think of the expense!*

But in the few minutes we have on the phone, she tells me about her remembered love for trees and her mission to find exactly the right kind of trees to plant in her front yard.

She knows the decision to plant a tree should not be taken lightly, so she studies the yards around town to see what everyone else is growing. It turns out that Mrs. Schnable, down the street, has a tree that Mom could imagine in her yard. Full wide branches. Pink blossoms in the spring. Imagine. *Pink blossoms.*

My mother waits to catch Mrs. Schnable out in the yard weeding her garden to ask, "What kind of tree is that?"

"A cherry tree," Mrs. Schnable says.

"I really like it," my mother says. "Where did you buy it?"

"I didn't buy it," Mrs. Schnable says, "I started it from seed."

Then Mrs. Schnable proceeds to tell my mother the most incredible story about how every year she took a cherry pit outside—one cherry pit—and dropped it into a hole and covered it with dirt, then waited through the summer, fall, winter, and spring to see if a sapling emerged.

I mean, who does that?

For quite a few years, nothing happened, Mrs. Schnable explains. But then after about seven or eight years of trying, finally one cherry pit took root. And now, my mother reports, Mrs. Schnable's cherry tree is luxurious, wide and tall.

"Who stays in one place year after year watching to see if one cherry pit takes root?" I ask.

"I know," she says, "I don't have that kind of time. I'm 79."

My mother has outlived everyone from her childhood now and almost everyone from her early adulthood, so talk of mortality doesn't make her uncomfortable. One Christmas when I called to say I couldn't brave another snowstorm to get home to North Dakota for the holidays, she warned me, "Well, you better visit soon. Because we're all dropping like flies up here."

So instead of going with the cherry-pit-in-the-hole method, my mother visits the Earl May Nursery in Bismarck. She no longer drives her own car to Bismarck—because of the stop lights and the traffic congestion and all—so she takes the Senior's Community Bus that goes around to all the small towns and transports people to the big city of Bismarck for shopping and doctor's appointments. My mother gets dropped off at Earl May and chooses two fledging trees, and our family friend, Mike Gibson, is dispatched to Bismarck with Dad's old pickup later that week to pick up the saplings.

Next time I talk to her, the trees have already been planted, and my mother is telling me how she loves to set the hose in the soil near the trunk and watch the water go down and down and down into the roots. They are very thirsty.

"What kind of trees did you get?" I ask.

"Oh, just wait," she says, searching for the tag from the nursery. "Ash," she reads, after a few seconds, "Green Ash."

A strange flutter starts up in my stomach.

"Fast growers," she says. "They told me they grow fast."

Why? Why? I stay silent on the other end of the line.

I live in Iowa, but I spend my summers in Kalamazoo, Michigan a few hours away from Canton, near Detroit, identified as ground-zero for the first sighting of the emerald ash borer (EAB) in 2002. This invasive beetle, believed to have traveled to North America in wood pallets from China, has spread in a shotgun blast perimeter out from eastern Michigan in all directions across many miles and states.

A tiny metallic green pest—about 1/2 inch long and 1/8 inch wide—with a bright red upper abdomen that can be seen when its wings spread, the emerald ash borer has been surprisingly destructive. Because ash trees were planted *en masse* precisely for their fast-growing quality when elms succumbed to Dutch Elm Disease in the '50s and '60s, it's no exaggeration to say that North America is now like a Chinese takeout buffet for the EAB.

A few summers earlier in my Michigan backyard as I was eyeing my tree line to see if I had ash trees, I began to talk with my next-door neighbors about the first house they bought as newlyweds near Detroit. They told me how they'd visited the house with the realtor and had fallen in love with it, largely because of the neighborhood's old canopies of shade trees overarching the streets. They put in the offer and got the house, and when they returned three months later to move in, the entire neighborhood had been stripped bare of trees—all ashes, all cut down because they were infected with emerald ash borer.

Since 2002, the emerald ash borer has killed tens of millions of trees and spread across twenty-five states and two Canadian provinces. The USDA has employed meticulous efforts to slow or stop its progress—sacrificing corridors of healthy ashes, creating buffer zones, policing natural barriers like the Mississippi River to keep the EAB from jumping, and enforcing the transportation of firewood across state lines. Despite these efforts, the ash borer has defied containment.

Both the adults and the larvae of the emerald ash borer feed on parts of the ash, but the larvae—flat, creamy-white, legless worms—do the real damage to the cambium under the bark, leaving the trunks with curving pathways of scars known as "pipelines," that look like meandering oxbows of rivers running up and down the length of the trunk. They kill the tree by disrupting and robbing it of the flow of nutrients.

And then there's human error: one Michigan camper was stopped on an Iowa highway in 2007 with twenty-four bundles of firewood strapped to the top of his camper. Why transport firewood across state lines? Firewood is $4 a bundle no matter where you are, and the minimum fine for violating the firewood quarantine in Illinois is $500. Just, why?

Scientists estimate the EAB has the potential to wipe out the entire *Fraxinus* genus of elms on North America, an estimated 8.7 billion trees.

I mention none of this to my mother. Each time I talk on the phone with her, I say, *Uh huh*, and *Wow*, and *Oh my goodness* as she tells me about her two baby ash trees. How the saplings are growing fast. How they made it through the first winter just fine. The tiny green buds and shoots of leaves are sprouting. How she can already imagine the shade they will soon be making.

And, in those conversations, even though I have not yet been home to experience the beauty of these young ash trees, I fall in love with them a little, too. This is the way that beauty convinces us to love it, to protect it, to duplicate and perpetuate it.

Beauty "gives us a moment of instruction," Elaine Scarry writes in *On Beauty and Being Just*. "Something you did not hold to be beautiful suddenly turns up in your arms arrayed in full beauty." Scarry offers her own experience with coming to appreciate a single palm tree:

I had ruled out palm trees as objects of beauty and
then one day discovered I had made a mistake.
Suddenly I am on a balcony and its huge swaying
leaves are before me at eye level, arcing, arching,
waving, creating and breaking in the soft air, throwing
the yellow sunlight up over itself and catching it on the
other side.[1]

This is how beauty convinces us—not with trees, but with one
tree—in a way that is singular. Scarry writes: "When I used to say
the sentence (softly and to myself) 'I hate palms' or 'Palms are
not beautiful; possibly they are not even trees,' it was a composite
palm that I had somehow succeeded in making without even ever
having seen, close up, many particular instances."[2]

But now when she says, "I love palms," she knows that she is
thinking of that *particular* palm, that one convincing palm tree
that spoke to her for the entire genus with "its leaves barely moving, just opening and closing slightly as though breathing."[3]

I practice a strict need-to-know protocol when offering any information to my parents—a holdover from my teenage years that
has transferred to adulthood—so I wonder how long my mother
could have gone on blissfully unaware of the emerald ash borer, that miniature winged juggernaut that's swarming toward her
baby ash trees?

Here's my thinking: North Dakota is far north and remote
enough that it might take years before the county extension
agents alert the public strenuously enough to reach her attention.
My mother watches CNN, NBC, and FOX, but environmental
warnings are not the sort of thing that news networks report on.

---

[1] Elaine Scarry, *On Beauty and Being Just* (Princeton University Press, 1999), p. 16.
[2] Scarry, p. 19.
[3] Scarry, p. 20.

My mother forages online, but mostly for jokes, recipes, and funny pet videos. No one on her Facebook feed is likely to post articles about invasive species infestation.

In the end, it was my second-oldest sister who lives in Minnesota who broke the news: *You know, Mom,* there's an insect that feeds on the kinds of trees that are in your front yard.

Dammit, full disclosure. Dammit, the unerring honesty of siblings.

The EAB, my sister reported to my mother, was only one state away—already in Minnesota.

Why do I find this so distressing? I'm a champion of small things in nature—rabbits, moles, voles, raccoons and opossum, along with ants and bees, the true heroes of the planet.

But in my mind, trees are in another protected class, like nobility. I mean, just look at them. "Able to make oxygen, sequester carbon, fix nitrogen, distill water, accrue solar energy as fuel, make complex sugars into food, build soil, change with the seasons, create microclimates and self-replicate," the environmental architect, William McDonough writes.[4] They are an ecosystem unto themselves. McDonough argues that, to survive, humans must invent ways to biomimic all the sustainable strategies that trees and plants employ.

German scientist, Peter Wohlleben, the author of *The Hidden Life of Trees,* similarly reports his awe of trees from twenty years of working in forest ecology. No tree stands alone, Wohlleben writes. They live in interdependent communities, protecting their weakest members for their own collective protection.

Groves are connected, he reports, by complex interlacing root systems capable of shuttling water and nutrients from one tree to a neighboring tree in need. And they are further connected by a subterranean underworld of super-delicate mycorrhizal fungi attached to the roots that create vast subsoil neurological networks

---

[4] William McDonough, "Address to the Woods Hole Symposium", 2003.
https://mcdonough.com/writings/address-woods-hole-symposium/

spreading chemical information up to hundreds or even thousands of times the length of the roots.

What humans see on the surface is such a small part of the story of trees. Some trees will release bitter toxic tannins from their leaves to discourage chewing insects and some can send chemical signals like ethelyne, a warning gas, into the air to alert neighboring trees to coming pestilence. Other trees send sweet smells into the air to attract pollinators.

Equally amazing, Wohlleben reports in *The Hidden Life of Trees* that adult beech trees employ a "pedagogical strategy" of depriving their young of sunlight, limiting their growth under tall adult canopies for decades, restricting their light exposure to around 3 percent, which is barely enough photosynthesis to keep their bodies from dying.[5]

As a result, the inner woody cells of the young beech tree grow tiny and almost devoid of oxygen, which makes the branches flexible and resilient, resistant to breaking in storms, impervious to fungi because they have the ability to compartmentalize their wounds. This harsh parental upbringing insures a long healthy life to the beeches.

In the foreword to Wohlleben's *The Hidden Life of Trees*, Tim Flannery posits that one of the reasons we fail to comprehend the complexity of trees is that they live on a far different time scale than humans: "One of the oldest trees on Earth, a spruce in Sweden, is more than 9,500 years old. That's 115 times longer than the average human lifetime."[6]

My mother's ash trees are not likely to have such longevity, but she was pretty sanguine about their imminent demise when she learned of the march of the emerald ash borer.

"We'll see," she says. "We'll deal with it when it reaches us."

My mother is ninety now. She's witnessed the complete disappearance of the two generations above her—her parents and

---

[5] Peter Wohlleben, *The Hidden Life of Trees* (Greystone, 2015), p. 32.
[6] Tim Flannery, "Foreword," found in *The Hidden Life of Trees*, by Peter Wohlleben, p. vii.

grandparents. She's lost my father and her entire generation of friends, all of whom have passed from this earth. She's experienced the death of one child, my sister Judy, an unexpected loss, like a sandy foundation giving way under our feet.

But look at her. Still climbing ladders to clean the cobwebs out of corners. Adopting a homeless cat named Von Trapp with an orange coat and matching golden eyes from a pet shelter, and not bothering to change his name to Baby or Snook-Ums, but calling him Trapper, for short.

Through her windows kitty-corner from the church, she looks after the neighborhood kids with their loud yippy dogs and their bikes strewn in the yard. She's finally given up her job cleaning the Catholic church, but she continues to do clothing alterations—hemming prom dresses and repairing the endless streams of torn work shirts and jeans of the people in my hometown who leave their garments in plastic bags on the desk outside her front door, right next to the plaster statue of Jesus.

And all of this with her hair still jet black. How does she do it?

I acknowledge now that it's a rare gift to have a mother, seemingly indestructible, who lives to old age. To come to know this version of my mother—as friend and companion, no longer mother as disciplinarian or supervisor, as looming sequoia—has made the world so much sweeter. Her faith in these ash trees has given me the latest lesson of many that I have received from knowing her: the fragile world calls us to love it—for its beauty, for its need to be protected, for the company and shelter it offers.

And as long as we are able, we are obligated to love it back.

The ash trees are eleven years old now. The last time I visited my mother, she stood on her front lawn under their lush canopies while I packed my car.

She put her hand on the solid bark, the trunks wide enough now that I would not be able to span them with my fingers. "Do you believe this?" she marveled. "I never thought I'd live long enough to sit in the shade of these trees."

An eerie ringing sets off in my ears when she says this—my mother, quoting the ancient wisdom of Greeks without ever having read the ancient Greeks.

If you get lucky in life, my mother has taught me, there will be the shade of trees and people you love to sit with you in that shade. To worry about too much else is pointless.

Ephemera

The thing is, I'm trying to finish my novel, but the water keeps coming in the basement. Not the basement of the novel, but the basement of my fiancé's house in Michigan where I spend my summers.

It's a strange feeling to go downstairs during an intense July storm, just to unplug the computer, and notice that the beige carpet in the northeast corner of the bedroom that doubles as your writing room has darkened to a wet triangle. Stranger still, to watch the stain spread to shades of taupe and dirty chocolate in the next few minutes, moving under the desk, toward the floor lamp and file cabinets.

I don't begrudge water; it can go wherever it wants, but even at that moment, it struck me as wrong. Water should not be here, in the house, bypassing the maze of foundation walls and footings that architects designed centuries ago to keep the inside in and the outside out.

And even as I turned and closed the door behind me, I knew it was irrational to think that maybe I didn't need to bother my fiancé with this information—that this lovely ten-year-old house with vaulted ceilings and wood floors that we'd poured all of our savings into had sprung a leak.

He was out in the flash-flooded street anyway, trying to clear the woodchips from the storm drains that we'd watched flow into the streets from our neighbors' yards moments earlier. He was standing in thigh-high water flailing away with a garden rake as puffs of lightning flashed and popped around him. Despite his efforts, the flood water had advanced halfway up the lawn.

When you buy property, you stake a claim to a small spot on earth. You trim, prune, and beautify. You fortify and defend. If the usual intruders try to enter—ants, mice, crickets, thieves—fixes can be found. But when 3.18 inches of rain falls in twenty-three minutes in Kalamazoo, Michigan, and you are (as we found out later from the Drain Commissioner) the lowest and last house to drain out of the watershed, plus your property has the poor taste to sit on a clay seam, well then you're just screwed. Because once water has found its way into your house, it will always remember you. It will always find a way in.

The downstate part of Michigan is shaped like a human palm. Sometimes if you ask Michiganders where they're from, they'll look around, as if searching for a map or a piece of paper, then they'll just give up and raise their right hand as if swearing an oath and point to the spot on their palm where their town is located. Detroit, for instance, is in the eastern part of the state, close to the crook of the thumb. My fiancé's house is in the heel of the palm, in Kalamazoo, in a direct line below the little finger.

The upper peninsula of Michigan also resembles a human palm, which people will sometimes demonstrate by hovering their other hand horizontally like a cumulus cloud over the vertical downstate palm. A few years ago, some guy made millions of dollars when he had the ingenious idea to make oven mitts with the upstate and downstate maps of Michigan printed on each hand. I'm not sure what became of him—the oven-mitt million-aire—but I've wondered if he has since retired to gentler climes, as Robert James Waller did after he wrote *The Bridges of Madison County*, then quit his job as a college professor in Iowa and re-tired to a spacious ranch in Texas.

Now that I spend part of the year in Michigan in a house that takes in water, I've observed that the state is also a peninsu-la, surrounded on three sides by the Great Lakes, which is why Michigan is sometimes called The Fourth Coast.

If not for dependable Ohio and a few stubborn sand-dune miles of Indiana, Michigan would be an island, floating unteth-ered like a lily pad in the filmy marsh upon which the state un-doubtedly rests.

Lately I've been making the mistake of watching The History Channel, or, as I like to call it—Countdown to the End Times. It was better when they stuck to real history like the hydrolog-ical marvels of Roman engineering, or even speculative history, like the search for Sasquatch across centuries and continents. But now The History Channel only seems intent on reporting the end of the world, based on the predictions of Nostradamus and the Mayan calendar.

It's unsettling to watch some sober plate-tectonic scientist from UC Berkeley speculate on how it might unfold, accompa-nied by animated graphics to simulate how the earth's crust is like an orange peel, and how it could someday, perhaps someday soon (and almost certainly has done so several times in the planet's history) just rotate and rearrange itself over the molten core of the earth, landing Florida in Antarctica, Moscow in Idaho, Bei-jing in the Arctic Circle.

My first impulse a few years ago when I heard the dire predictions for 2012, was to say, "My God, I have to finish my book projects!" Then it dawned on me, "Wait, if the world is going to end, it doesn't *matter* if I finish my books, because no one will be around to read them." So we may as well spend what short time we have hanging out with friends, cooking, making love, drinking wine, as the Epicureans advised us to do so many centuries ago.

I've decided if the end of the world comes, I'm going as fast as I can, not to my fiancé's house in the floating palm of Michigan where I spend my summers, or even to Iowa where I live and work during the school year. As solid seeming as it appears, Iowa sits atop a mid-continent rift buried deep in the bedrock, a billion-year-old tectonic scar that stretches from Lake Superior to Kansas.

Instead, I'm running back to my home state of North Dakota, to the terra firma of my childhood, where I'm convinced nothing bad can happen. (Besides, I've seen my brother's gun collection.) Or I'm going to Greece, where people have already demonstrated they can hang onto the cliffs and hillsides like billy goats for millennia and survive.

The novel I'm writing about Greece is narrated from the perspective of an outsider. The idea first came to me in 1998 after I returned from my first trip to Athens and Corfu with my then-husband, who is Greek-American, and whose maternal and paternal grandparents immigrated to the United States in the 1940s from different parts of Greece.

Upon our return, after our rolls of film were developed, I was surprised to discover that I had taken very few pictures of people—not the dozens of his friendly relatives who had appeared at the hotel each day in exponentially multiplying numbers. I had not taken pictures of the beautiful tables of food they prepared for us, which we ate in their marble-floored dining rooms or in the seaside cafés around the islands that they took us to, where we talked and laughed and drank wine as the sun dropped like an orange ball extinguishing itself into the Ionian.

Nor had I photographed the narrow, cobbled streets we drove through to get to those cafés, or the little shops full of t-shirts and curios we walked past, or the white sandy beaches and misty harbors with sailboats, nor even the Venetian forts overlooking the port or the tan hills in the distance.

Instead, I had shot roll after roll of olive trees, groves of them, up and down the terraced landscapes—each tree flashing green then silver in the wind, each one looking so unique and wizened, so human-looking, I suppose, that it must have felt when I came upon them, that I was seeing old friends who must be remembered with a photograph.

In Greece, people will sometimes say, "This olive tree was alive at the time of Christ," or "This tree witnessed the fall of the Roman Empire," but it's still uncertain exactly how old olive trees can live to be. On the island of Crete, there's evidence on the basis of tree ring analysis of a 2,000 year-old olive tree with suspicion that it's much older. Several olive trees in the Middle East and Mediterranean (around Greece and in Croatia, Italy, Palestine, and Israel) have been identified as 2,000 years old or older. One tree in West Athens is referred to as "Plato's olive tree," because it's believed to mark the last vestiges of a grove where Plato's Academy stood 2,400 years ago. Olive trees were mentioned in Homer and by Pliny the Elder.

As an American, it's hard for me to think in these long timescapes, but evidence of the ancient is everywhere present in modern-day Greece. Traveling around, it's not unusual for someone to point to an opening in a rock face and say, "See, right there, that's the cave where Zeus was reared," or "That's where Persephone was dragged down into Hades."

Really, you want to say, God, I thought that was myth.

On my first trip to Greece, we were rushed around the island of Corfu by my husband's relatives. Everyone needed to be satisfied that we had been shown the expected sites—the gaudy Achilleion Palace built by Emperor Franz Josef for his wife, and the spare sarcophagus of St. Spyridon in Corfu Town.

The haste with which we were dispatched, signaled to us that his relatives had done this a million times. They even knew the best places for us to pose—"Here, stand here"—they'd prop us in front of a rocky outcropping, a blooming trellis of bougainvillea, a marble statue. *Click, click.*

"Good." They'd grab us by the shoulders. "Now, let's go eat."

Then they drove us to Palaiokastritsa, a headland on the western shore of the island of Corfu with a monastery and a cliff overlooking a bay that had the most aquamarine water I had ever seen, and as I was looking down upon the water in stunned silence my husband's cousin, Nick, pointed to a tiny island of rock just yards off the coast.

"Do you remember how the Phaeacians helped Odysseus return to Ithaca?" he asked.

I combed through my dim memories of *The Odyssey*, then ventured a guess. "They showered him with gifts, then sailed him home?"

"Yes," he said. "Then Poseidon punished them by changing the ship and its sailors to stone."

Oh sure, I nodded, as if I'd recalled these details all along.

"Well?" He said and pointed a crooked finger expectantly at the tiny rock island. "That's it—right there. That's the stone boat."

Wow, *really*, I thought that was myth?

In February of 1956, around the time I was conceived in a farmhouse on a hill in the high plains of North Dakota, the temperature in the Mediterranean fell to an unprecedented low of -7°C, causing a winter kill in olive groves around the region considered to be "the worst calamity since record-keeping began in 1739." In his book, *Olives*, Mort Rosenblum reports that "the trunks of olive trees froze and exploded." Ancient family groves were decimated. Millions of olive trees perished.

This catastrophe coincided with the event of my conception, so maybe this is why these two places—North Dakota and Greece—are entwined inside me in ways I can't yet explain. Maybe this is why, when I was on the island of Lesvos during the winter of 2002 to research olive groves and work on my novel set in Greece, I spent each day feverishly writing—not about Greece, but about my home state of North Dakota. Even at the time, it made no sense to me, as I sat in my rented studio tucked into the steep hillside in Molyvos with views out the window near my writing desk overlooking the cascade of terra cotta roofs descending down the mountainside to a blue patch of the Aegean. Through the other window in the far distance was the feathered silhouette of Mount Lepetimnos, and all I could think and write about was the cold, flat, austere beauty of North Dakota.

Traveling in Greece, I've been fascinated by the guidebook entries for each island, the running summary of the waves of oppressors who have vanquished the very ground upon which you are now standing. The tour guide will point to the evidence of the conquerors in the local architecture, the vestiges of city walls, the location of the moat, the style of construction of the stone streets, the fortifications on the hillside.

Each in their own time the Romans, Venetians, Ottomans, and in the last century the Turks, Germans, and Italians have taken their turns colonizing the place, but here's the thing that gives me hope: it's the Greeks, still there, still pointing to the architectural remnants, ruins, and battlements.

And it is olive trees that most remind me that things go on beyond the small measure of a human life—the vegetative equivalent of long geological time, the reason that some people visit gorges and canyons or mountain ranges, to feel inspired by the immensity.

When you come into the presence of sacred places, N. Scott Momaday writes, "You touch the pulse of the living planet. You feel its breath upon you. You become one with a spirit that pervades geologic time, that indeed confounds time and space." Momaday writes, "When I stand on the edge of Monument Valley and behold the great red and blue and purple monoliths floating away in the distance, I have the certain sense that I see beyond time. There the earth lies in eternity."[7]

So I spend summers now in a house in Michigan that has two sump pumps—one on the southeast corner and one in the northwest corner. We call it The Boathouse. I don't imagine we'll ever be able to sell it. Sometimes we talk to our neighbors over the fence and declare in voices sounding like Ma and Pa Kettle, "Nosiree, Bob, we're not leaving. We'll defend this clay seam 'til we die."

To fix the water problem, we had to hire a crew to come in and jackhammer out the interior perimeter of the basement foundation so that the crew could lay a drain tile system underneath the house and install the sumps. After the pipes were laid and fixed in place, they cemented the basement floor back over so that aside from a bit of discoloration in the concrete, you'd never notice. But it's alarming to have crews in your basement for three days with jackhammers billowing great clouds of gypsum upstairs, then to watch them lug huge chunks of your foundation up the staircase and out to the dump truck.

---

[7] N. Scott Momaday, *The Man Made of Words: Essays, Stories, Passages* (St. Martin's Press, 1997), p. 114.

And it's disconcerting after the crew leaves for the day to go downstairs and catch a glimpse of the very earth that rests under your house. It's something you think you should never see, maybe like seeing the mass of gray matter inside your skull while watching your own brain surgery on closed-circuit television.

So the drains are installed now under the foundation, capturing the water that seeps around the crease of the footings, and the pipes carry the water to the sumps, which spit it back out of the house in one efficient flush into the yard. We had back-up batteries installed on the sump pumps as a fail-safe, so if the power goes out they will continue to function.

It only took us two years and about $20,000 to figure all this out. Still, when it rains we get twitchy. We stick close to home. We spend way too much time watching The Weather Channel.

For extra peace of mind, last year for Father's Day, I bought my fiancé a gas generator large enough to power a small city. So if the power goes out (which it frequently does in Michigan) and the backup batteries fail, we can always fire up the generator, which is louder than a chopped-out Harley. Tom rolls it out on the driveway and fires it up for a few minutes each month. When he comes back inside, he says, "Our neighbors must hate us."

I remember the day we stood in the aisle of Home Depot with all the other bearded and tattooed Michiganders who were shopping for generators that weekend. "We're preparing for the end times," we kept saying, as a joke. You could tell it didn't seem funny to anyone else.

Olive groves are not planted by short-sighted people. Depending upon the species, olive trees take from seven to seventeen years to bear first fruit. Some olive trees bear fruit for hundreds of years. The investment is in a future one is not likely to live to enjoy.

The entire history of the development of Mediterranean cultures has been tied by ethno-botanists to the spread of the olive tree. In *A Prospero's Cell: a Guide to the Landscape and Manners of the Island of Corfu*, Lawrence Durrell notes that "the whole Mediterranean—the sculptures, the palms, the gold beads, the bearded heroes, the wine, the ideas, the ships, the moonlight, the winged gorgons, the bronze men, the philosophers—all of it seems to rise in the sour, pungent taste of these black olives between the teeth." It is a "taste older than meat, older than wine," Durrell writes, "a taste as old as cold water."

In the origin story of the city of Athens, a competition is held between Athena and Poseidon for the right as protector of the city. Each god offered a gift—Poseidon struck his trident on the ground and created a spring; Athena threw a spear from which an olive tree grew. The tree won the favor of the king, and so, fortunately, the city is called Athens and not Poseidonia.

The fruits of the olive tree can be tied to every human need, from physical to spiritual—as an oil for heating and cooking as well as to light votive offering-lamps; as an emollient for the skin. It took humans a relatively long time to figure out how to use olives as a food supply, but the discovery was significant. Scholars theorize that Alexander the Great was able to march and conquer lands at such great distances in part because the curing of olives provided his armies with a portable food supply.

At one time, Greek infants were given an olive branch at birth; athletes were awarded olive branches and an amphora of olive oil for success in competition. Olives and olive trees are mentioned over thirty times in the Bible—most notably in Genesis 8:11, in the story of the Great Flood: "When the dove returned to him in the evening, there in its beak was a freshly plucked olive leaf! Then Noah knew that the water had receded from the earth." In this story, as in most stories about olives and olive trees, the leaf serves as irrefutable proof of hospitable climate, the possibilities for habitation.

"Wittgenstein says that when the eye sees something beautiful, the hand wants to draw it," Elaine Scarry observes in *On Beauty and Being Just*. In this way, beauty "brings copies of itself into being." The impulse to reproduce beauty is likely tied to biological imperative—"beauty prompts a copy of itself"—but it extends, Scarry argues, to all forms of beauty: flora, fauna, landscape.[8]

In the case of Greece, which tempts writers and artists with its beauty, it also eludes them, because Greece cannot be reduced to broad strokes—a glass of ouzo on a white terrace, some Rembetiko music, and the tinkle of a goat's bell in the distance. The closer you look, the more its complexities mushroom. The artist is doomed to fail, which is why we have enough paintings of sunlit beaches and sailboats on the Aegean and enough books about flings with dark-haired men and the-summer-of-my-Greek-Taverna to last an eternity, or at least until 2012.

As an artist who wishes to write a narrative about this place I have come to love, I fear this guarantee of failure, even before I've begun. The main character in my novel is a stranger and not expected to be conversant in the language, religion, botany, myths, geology, geography, history, and politics of the place; yet, I must know them. And there's another problem: cultural theft. Greece is a place from which much has been stolen.

I have stood in the new Acropolis Museum in Athens under the temporary frieze created by architect, Bernard Tschumi, that highlights the travesty of the missing Elgin Marbles—more than half of the Parthenon frieze, the metopes and pediments that Lord Elgin claimed as an archeological treasure for the British Museum two centuries ago when he served as British ambassador to the Ottoman Empire, and which the Greeks have requested and demanded countless times to be returned to Athens.

---

[8] Scarry, *On Beauty and Being Just*, p. 3.

The Acropolis Museum display, described in a *New York Times* article by Michael Kimmelman as a "$200 million, 226,000-square-foot, state-of-the-art rebuttal to Britain's argument," wraps around the top floor of the museum in a room otherwise filled with light.[9] In the Acropolis Museum display, one can circle the entire perimeter of the frieze and see the original fragments—the ones Lord Elgin chose for whatever reason to leave behind. These weathered fragments of the original marble are installed in the permanent frieze to duplicate the way it would have looked when mounted on the Parthenon. In the empty spaces where the stolen sections belong, the museum has installed rough and chalky white plaster replicas of the originals from the British Museum that painfully demonstrate their absence and their rightful place.

If you are a person of conscience, to circle that room for any amount of time, to mingle with Greeks as they circle and look up at where the marble ends and the plaster begin, is to feel the weight of the hand of power on you, to feel the audacity of theft that imperialism allows and perpetuates. It causes one to want to incite violence. It also causes a confusion to rise up in me—helplessness, then guilt and anger, then complicity.

I begin to worry in new ways about my small project, which lays its own unrightful claim to the riches of Greece. I study and worry, study and worry. Will I ever develop enough fluency in the place to earn a right to finish my novel set in Greece?

To calm myself, I return to the subject of olive trees: If you grew up on an island in Greece, let's say Lesvos, in a house that bordered an olive grove. Let's not say it's an ancient grove. Let's say it's four hundred years old, conservatively. And if you had picked

[9] Michael Kimmelman, "Elgin Marble Argument in a New Light," *The New York Times*, June 23, 2009.

olives each year, and if your parents had picked olives from that same grove and had cooked with the oil, and their parents had picked from the grove and made oil and used the oil for cooking and for lamps and as an emollient, and if you assumed or knew for certain that their parents and their parents and their parents, going back those four hundred years, conservatively, had done the same—then how would that shape the way you felt about the house and the grove, about the village down the side of the hill, and about the people you met on that path each day?

And let's just say there arose some dispute over the ownership of that olive grove, because a place that has spawned so many generations will naturally have to cast off members to preserve equilibrium, to send them to the city or to other countries. And so let's say one of those disgruntled cast-off family members decides to circle back home and take a torch to the grove of olive trees, so that the land can be cleared and be made available for lucrative sale to Germans or Dutch retirees or for development as a resort for tourists.

If this were to happen in a wheat field or corn field even on a midwestern Century Farm in the United States, the offense would be serious, but it might be recoverable. But if it happens to a four-hundred-year-old olive grove, what is the equivalent seriousness of the crime committed against the land and the family? I don't know these answers, but they are questions that writing the novel is making me ask.

Geologists tell us that the two primary shapers of landscape are wind and water. I was shaped by a flat, landlocked place. Windy and recently glaciated, it was devoid of water. Sometimes I think that the flood water in the floating palm of Michigan was trying to school me, to teach me something about itself when it came into the basement.

And if I'd only paid attention, rather than worrying so much about the carpet and the collection of junk in cardboard boxes that I was too lazy and noncommittal to throw away, I may have learned enough to write about it, would have finished the novel already, and the water would have gone elsewhere—into the street, into the storm drains, into another neighbor's basement, into the riverbeds, on its way to Lake Michigan.

And now it's well past 2012 already, and I can just imagine that big blue water bag of the lake bulging and breaking, ready to submerge the state of Michigan once and for all. Or I can imagine the big seamy gorge of the Mississippi River, the way it could split the continent down the center if the earth's crust decided to shrug us off a bit, and it gets me wondering what the true purpose of all this scholarly activity is. These books we compose, and the thousands of hours we invest in the writing and reading of them. What is their value when compared to the true currency of another day on earth, another twenty-four hours to be healthy and alive? To breathe, to sing, to eat, kiss, make love.

These utterances, this breath that flows through the vessels of our bodies shaped into words and songs, into chants and prayers, curses and gossip that we convert to scribblings, to something we imagine might stay put—what does it all amount to? And who will ever care to remember it, ever remember to read it?

A horse can live to be forty; a camel, fifty. A queen bee might get five good years, while a worker bee is lucky to have one. The amazon parrot can make it to one hundred years, and the Galapagos land tortoise can live 190 plus, under optimal conditions. An elephant has about forty years; an American alligator, fifty-six.

And Athena's tree from mythic time—the one that grew out of the spear she threw to defeat Poseidon and earn the honor of namesake of Athens—was reputed to have lived for thousands of years by the temple of Pandrosus near the Parthenon. During the Persian Wars, after Xerxes defeated Athens in 480 BC and ordered the city to be razed, all that remained of Athena's tree was a blackened stump. Yet Herodotus claims that soon after the flames were doused, a green shoot sprang from the dead stump out of which grew an olive tree that survived to the second century AD—demonstrating the promise of generation and regeneration even after great catastrophe.

What do humans get? One irreplaceable unit of time, averaged out between genders in the United States, likely to last about 77.9 years. We are fragile creatures, short in our time on earth, especially when matched against the fierce power of the cosmologies, the long temporal landscapes, and the rougher geologies of the planet.

This ephemeral life. Just when it starts to get really interesting, that's when it becomes clear that someday, perhaps someday soon, we will have to close our eyes and look no more upon it—the awful beauty of the world.

Those Desirable Things

Considering that Mary Carmichael was no genius, but an unknown girl writing her first novel in a bed-sitting-room, without enough of those desirable things, time, money, and idleness, she did not do so badly, I thought. . . . Give her a room of her own and five hundred a year, let her speak her mind and leave out half that she now puts in, and she will write a better book one of these days.

—Virginia Woolf, *A Room of One's Own*

My copy of *A Room of One's Own* is old, purchased used in the bookstore of the university I attended in the 1980s. In the years since, it's been pushed deep into the corner of the shelf by other books—Rich, Lorde, Kristeva, Cixous. A small book, it holds down the dusty edge.

"Non-Required" is stamped on the inside front cover, along with the price—$2.95. I would have browsed it out of the shelves that afternoon in the '80s, in search of something inexpensive to buy, so that I would have an excuse to write a check for forty dollars cash above the amount of purchase. Then I would take the forty dollars, exit the bookstore, and drive straight to the bank to deposit it.

This mysterious behavior was part of a shell game I played sometimes near the end of my two-week pay period. Back then, when checks took two days to clear the bank, I might go to two or three businesses, writing checks for whatever amount of cash was allowable above the small purchase I'd make, then cobble all the cash together and deposit it in the bank before 3:00 p.m. Thus, that day's cash covered the checks I'd written (probably for cash to deposit) two days earlier, and in this way, I would leapfrog—check, cash, check, cash—buying myself a few extra days until payday mercifully arrived. I spent many lunch breaks doing this.

Once at home, at the end of my workday, I would have taken the book upstairs to my bedroom—not a room of my own at all, not even a bed-sitting-room—but a bedroom in an apartment I shared with my guitar-player boyfriend. I had a small desk in one corner for my scribbled poems and a wobbling tower of milk crates full of books in the corner behind the door.

My boyfriend and I had moved back to this college town when our heavy metal road band had broken up several months earlier. I was trying to reconstruct something of a life by taking graduate classes at night and working as a secretary at a construction company during the day to support us.

As a former rock and roll singer, I had some things to recommend me—a strong singing voice with a good sense of pitch, the ability to sleep well in moving vehicles, a silhouette that still looked passable in spandex and leather—but few of them marketable in the above-ground real world. However, I'd always been a fast typist. By some miracle, the office manager of the construction firm had hired me when I answered the ad.

I'm sorry to say, not much sex happened in that bedroom, and not much sleeping either. My boyfriend and I were both angry over the bad turn our music careers had taken, and we began to see each other only as painful reminders.

He spent most of his time in the sub-basement bedroom we had set up as his guitar studio. He was a classically trained pianist and guitarist, a composer, and an electric guitarist with three recorded albums. Somewhere along the way, we'd decided that he was the greater genius and more deserving of the space. He also had guitars, keyboards, and 100-watt Marshall amplifier stacks that had to be put somewhere. Besides, I told myself, poets and singers make art from the very air they breathe.

My boyfriend had taken to brooding long hours in his downstairs studio over the growing realization that he was not going to be a famous rock star. He spent his nights down there, practicing electric guitar, running his fingers up and down the neck practicing Dorian and Myxolidian scales to keep his chops up. At midnight, after I'd gone to bed, he'd switch to his classical guitar, moving through Segovia's full repertoire until the early hours. By the middle of the night, after everything went silent, he would labor away at the kitchen table on his *magnum opus*, an exhaustive manual of rock guitar instruction he had titled, "Chase the Dragon."

Eventually to make some money, he was forced to take on students—work that he informed me at every turn was beneath him. In the years that followed, I learned that much was beneath him—going to liquor stores to buy the wine and beer he enjoyed with dinner, going to grocery stores to buy food, cooking, cleaning, paying bills, talking with the landlord or anyone who wished to speak with us, filling gas, car repair. Let's just say I got to know a lot of mechanics.

In those late afternoons, after I got home from my office job, I would retire to our upstairs bedroom to read or prepare for my night classes while a steady stream of his guitar students made their way at half-hour intervals through our front door, through my kitchen and down the stairs to his studio, like ants on a food trail, I always thought.

As power chords and shrill guitar solos rang through the floorboards, I sat upstairs in the bedroom with the door closed, pillows propped behind my back, reading the big novels required for my classes—Hemingway, Fitzgerald, Faulkner, Tolstoy. In truth, I loved those novels, their largeness of scope and mastery of language, the way they delivered me, if only for a few hours, away from the realities of my immediate situation. No one had yet told me about what had become of Zelda.

So on that night, after the latest check-cashing excursion, I would have picked up *A Room of One's Own* only after all the required reading was complete. I must have read her sideways, out of the corner of one squeamish eye. It would have been too hard to look straight-on at her assertion "that it is necessary to have five hundred a year and a room with a lock on the door if you are to write fiction or poetry."[10]

Even allowing a generous margin for symbolism, that five-hundred-a-year stands for the power to contemplate, that lock on the door means the power to think for oneself; still you may say that a mind should rise above such things.

Re-reading my copy now, I see that I marked only two passages in the entire book. The first underlined passage reads, "A woman must have money and a room of her own if she is to write fiction; and that, as you will see, leaves the great problem of the true nature of woman and the true nature of fiction unsolved."[11]

As a dutiful student, I would have seen this as the central thesis and worth underlining. I also would have agreed with it. We'd been arguing with our professor about the absence of women authors on the "Great American Novels of the 20th Century" readings list. He had countered that there weren't comparable novels of quality by women from which to choose. Did Cather's books belong too much to the nineteenth century? Was Stein too experimental? Reading Woolf's imaginary account of Shakespeare's

---

[10] Virginia Woolf, *A Room of One's Own* (Harvest/HBJ, 1976), p. 105.
[11] Woolf, p. 4.

sister in *A Room of One's Own*, I wondered what had become of Updike's sister?

The second passage in the book that I marked deals with the difficulties any writer, despite gender, has to create what Woolf calls "a work of genius." She writes, "Generally material circumstances are against it. Dogs will bark; people will interrupt; money must be made; health will break down." The world doesn't care, Woolf continues, "whether Flaubert finds the right word."[12] Although no Flaubert, I would have seen myself in those words.

I had big aspirations, and a few ideas. How was I going to stoke this small ember? Reading on, I found grimmer news. When Woolf goes in search of the bookshelf on which the novels written by women are kept, she finds it empty. She concludes that beyond the formidable material difficulties women writers face, "much worse were the immaterial."[13]

The indifference of the world, which Keats and Flaubert and other men of genius have found so hard to bear, was in her case not indifference but hostility. The world did not say to her as it said to them, Write if you choose; it makes no difference to me. Instead, the world said with a guffaw, Write? What's the good of your writing?

I suppose at this point something steely rose up in me, a kind of backbone. I was a young woman, after all, who had dropped out of college in the '70s and broken up with a very nice, very rich fiancé to join a rock band. I had defied my parents and kicked around the West and parts of Canada for seven years, a woman traveling alone in vans full of male musicians, fronting hard rock and heavy metal bands, living by my wits and singing my lungs out every night.

---

[12] Woolf, p. 51–52.
[13] Woolf, p. 52.

Very soon, I moved my tower of books and my little desk down to the sub-basement laundry room that sat across the hallway from my boyfriend's guitar studio. It was no more than a closet, but it was empty because we didn't have a washer and dryer. (Did I mention that I spent lots of time at the Laundromat, watching towels and shirts, socks and men's underwear floating in circles?)

Months later, when the laundry room proved too claustrophobic, I went deeper, moving all my books and writing materials into the cement corner of the crawl space under the apartment. It was an open half-story that ran under the length and width of the main floor. To get around in it, you had to bend at the waist. Each night, I would duck-walk my way to my desk, then sit down on a short stool over which a bare bulb hung. In that underground space under a ceiling that grazed a few inches above my head, I worked on my first poems and stories.

My boyfriend, cozy in his studio space, viewed all this settling and re-settling of my writing space as my perpetual fussing over things instead of getting down to the business of doing them. Never mind. I was on the move, my writing room was on the move, and the room inside me was on the move. Soon, the walls would break open.

Weeks later, in response to an assignment to write a short story, I sat down at the kitchen table in the late afternoon with a yellow legal pad while all those guitar students came and went, playing their tormented scales and solos downstairs. And in one fevered exhalation, I wrote a fifteen-page treatise on what it had felt like to be a singer. It began with the lines, "In the third grade, I did very well in the screaming auditions for *Hansel and Gretel*. I got to be the witch." It wasn't fiction, but I didn't care.

The next day, on the sneak when I was supposed to be typing up financial reports at the construction company where I worked, I typed up my story on my work computer, putting them down just as the words had appeared on the hand-written page. And I printed it up on the company's printer, then ran multiple copies for distribution to my class on the construction firm's copy machine during the lunch hour when my boss was away. My petty larceny was growing. I had become a photocopy thief for my art.

The next week, when we workshopped it in class, my teacher said something astonishing, something I'd never heard in a workshop before. He said, "It's finished. Send it out." So I did, the next week, using postage stamps from my construction company's office desk drawer, and three months later I got the letter in the mail, telling me that my essay had won a prize, had been selected by Philip Lopate, and that it would be published. Imagine.

Seeing this modest book on my shelf all these years later, I realize I've been slow to acknowledge the role that Woolf's words played in my own transformation. Although back then I could only bear a sideways glance at her words, they emboldened me. And even now, each day that I write with my own paper, on my own computer, in my own well appointed writing room, I try to construct sentences from a state of mind that she wished for all of us—one that is "resonant and porous . . . creative, incandescent and undivided."

If, as Woolf suggests, women writers should lay a wreath on the graves of Jane Austen and George Eliot, and "let flowers fall upon the tomb of Aphra Behn," then what magnificent bouquet, with what massive and impossibly-tied ribbon should go to Woolf?[14]

I don't believe she would have wanted it. Such fanfare would have startled and embarrassed her. Soon after, I can imagine her going upstairs to write in her journal: "Gardenias arrived this morning; pallor white & large as hotcakes; sweet sick smell fills the room, told L. to put them out."

---

[14] Woolf, *A Room of One's Own*, p. 66.

Living to Tell the Tale

The seats on the Yak-40, the Yakovlev airplane, that I caught out of Odessa to escape the Ukrainian heat that August of 1998 were threadbare and wire-sprung as old movie theater cushions. Spanning three across on either side of the aisle, the seats were sloped and indented as if still bearing the weight of the legions of asses that had previously risked flying Odessa Airlines.

The overhead compartments were not the cover-and-latch design that you see in modern airplanes, but instead were simple open ledges with a ropy mesh enclosure strung across the front to keep packages from falling during flight. No matter. Instead of luggage, many of my fellow passengers, mostly Ukrainians and Russians, carried their belongings in paper shopping bags or cardboard boxes strapped together with duct tape worked into loops for handles.

On the list of regional airlines that the *Lonely Planet Guide* advised tourists to avoid when traveling in Russia and Ukraine, the name of Odessa Airlines was not even included. Perhaps that's because the airline, with its fleet of three aircraft, fell below even negative consideration. And maybe that's why Odessa Airlines had the only seats to Moscow available when my translator, Pavel, had inquired about a last-minute flight for me that morning.

None of this occurred to me until after I'd surrendered my Ukrainian travel visa to customs inside the Odessa Airport. The female customs official, who was heavily-mascaraed and belted mercilessly into her deep blue uniform with canary epaulets, studied my photo against my flushed face for what felt like long minutes before returning my passport to me with her right hand and separating away with her left hand my stamped travel visa, depositing it into a slim and irretrievable drop slot on her countertop.

After this, there was nothing to do but file through the glass doors of the Odessa Airport with the other travelers, past orange pylons and vertical concrete barriers to be emptied out onto the tarmac and into the harsh brilliance of the 120°F afternoon.

Around me, heat vapors streamed and wavered in expanding and contracting vertical spires. All you could do was stand and sweat. It didn't pay to fan yourself. Fanned air was as hot as forced heat. Mirages of aquamarine floated on the near horizon like pools of water. The bituminous gas from the runway's soft tar rose acrid to my nostrils, singeing my eyes.

I turned back to wave goodbye one last time to my translator, who watched me now from behind the airport windows, his long, serious Moldovan face appearing even more grim, more worried than it had grown in the last few days as he'd watched my health deteriorate.

I'd arrived a week earlier, a healthy American woman on a six-week family history roots pilgrimage that had already taken me from Paris to Strasbourg, France to Munich, first visiting the small villages along the Rhine River where my ancestors were originally from. In Odessa, Pavel had assisted me in visiting the villages thirty kilometers northwest of Odessa on the Black Sea that my Alsatian ancestors had immigrated to in 1803 when they fled the violence of the French Revolution and answered an invitation for free land from the Russian Tsar, Alexander I.

For over seventy-five years, they'd prospered in these villages they created along the Black Sea, then part of Russia, before fleeing the region for America in the years leading up to the Russian Revolution. All of my great-grandparents and my two grandfathers, as children, eventually immigrated to the Dakota Territory between the years of 1886 and 1911, and it had been my crazy aim on this research trip to retrace the migration paths of my ethnic group, otherwise known as Germans-from-Russia.

To keep things interesting, I also planned to track down the descendants of siblings that my great-grandparents had left behind in Russia—distant relatives who had lived through the depredations following the Revolution such as forced starvation and farm collectivization. When Stalin declared members of my ethnic group enemies of the state during World War II, they were all shipped to labor camps in Siberia.

For the next three weeks, according to my original itinerary, I was to leave Odessa by train to Moscow for a three-day stay with a Russian family; then on to western Siberia via the Trans-Siberian railroad to meet academic colleagues I'd met through correspondence in Omsk who would help me find translators and transportation to visit remote villages near Novosibirsk and Tomsk, where I hoped to find people from my ethnic group, perhaps some of them distant relatives, who had eventually migrated there after Khrushchev revoked their "enemy" status after Stalin's death in 1956.

It was a complicated history, and a complicated plan that had been a year in the making. And now I was jettisoning everything, boarding a plane for Moscow, and abandoning my trip because of weather.

In the six days I'd been in Odessa, the temperatures hovered between 120°F during the day and 100°F in the evening. From my sea-view room on the eighth floor of the Chernoye More

Hotel on Rishelyevskaya Street, I watched the harbor waters of the Black Sea steam and mist in the port overlooking the Potemkin Steps. Crows swooped from roof to roof then landed on the wrought iron of the faux balcony outside my window in the middle of the night, calling out to each other in ominous caws. Although the Chernoye More boasts a four-star rating with many promised conveniences, air conditioning was not one of them. In fact, it was not possible to find a fully-functioning air conditioner in any hotel or restaurant in the city of Odessa.

That morning, a week into my stay in Odessa, Pavel had arrived as usual to pick me up at my hotel for another day of field research. I told him that I'd decided to cancel the rest of my trip. I'd already spent the previous day in an Odessa hospital—undergoing tests and eventually discharging myself against doctor's orders—with a diagnosis of heat stroke. Over the last week, I'd begun having trouble calling phone numbers and calculating time differences and currency. I couldn't put sentences together. I hadn't slept; I wasn't keeping food down. I lost ten pounds in five days.

And if I thought I might get relief by getting out of Odessa on the train to Moscow in two days according to my original plan, I was mistaken. The night before, I'd met two women who had come in by train in this same oppressive weather from Yalta on the Crimean Peninsula. They told me their first-class tickets hadn't counted for anything. There was no air conditioning in any cars of the train. People on the trains were gravely ill from the heat, and the windows of your car may open, or they may be sealed shut and deadly hot inside.

"If only your ancestors could so easily have canceled their trip to Siberia," Pavel said, after I told him my plans. Then he got on the phone to look for a flight to Moscow for me later that day.

After I leave the tarmac and climb the steep air ladder with the wobbly handrail connected to the exterior of the plane, I find the interior comfortably shady and cool at first. I walk down the aisle and find a section of seats all for myself. I stash my backpack of research books under the window seat and stretch out my legs on the steel-gray, dirty-blue décor of the Yak-40 that is more reminiscent of a 1970s Greyhound than an airplane.

As my fellow passengers board, they stow their bags overhead. Across the aisle from me in the window seat is a very young, very tall and thin, very blond man in an impeccable black suit with fashionable black eyeglasses. I imagine he's a Russian businessman.

As we wait for the passengers to board, the flight attendants, to break the heat, move through the cabin offering small glasses of chilled champagne poured into ornate plastic champagne flutes. I take them up on several pours as they come and go.

For the record, to try to sit, move, sleep, or function in 120°F without the benefit of even momentary air conditioning is not to experience heat so much as claustrophobia, as if suspended inside a bubble of molten amber or like being slowly smothered to death by a very large, very hairy bear.

If my plan was to escape the heat, I have not succeeded. It's broiling on the plane. The fans are not working as the plane waits on the hot runway for the passengers to board with the engines off. I avail myself of another glass of bubbly champagne to cool off. Maybe because I haven't kept any food down for days or maybe because I was dehydrated before I boarded, I am quickly drunk and feeling morose. I sag in my saggy seat and begin to weep openly.

The Russian businessman monitors me, as do the three men in the row in front of me who swivel their heads to almost glance at me in response to my nose-blowing and muffled sobs. But their interest is trained mostly on the Styrofoam cooler they have carried onto the plane that's now wedged snuggly between their legs on the floor in front of their seats. It's full of ice and many cool beers. One of them turns and offers me a sweaty bottle. *No, thanks.* I sob and shake my head. *Never mind*, I think to myself. *This plane is going down.*

I'm a poet, not a journalist. But I'm guessing that one of the first rules of journalism is to avoid becoming part of the story you are trying to report. As soon as I landed in Odessa a week earlier, I could feel myself losing control of the story, crossing over that line.

On that day of my arrival, after I de-boarded, I felt the heat. And especially after I picked up my luggage and entered the Odessa Airport terminal, I felt panic as a mob of freelance drivers descended upon me offering rides.

I had just come from three weeks in Western Europe where all I had to do was keep my mouth shut and I was able to pass as a local in France and Germany. French teenagers had even rushed up to me near the Eiffel Tower and asked for directions. Imagine their surprise when I turned and said to them in English, "I'm lost, too."

Now, in Odessa, everything about me—my dress, jewelry, hairstyle, luggage, body language—apparently marked me as an American. I have always been an intrepid solitary traveler, an old rock and roll musician who traveled with road bands all over the country in the 1970s and '80s, but now, I realized, I was in too deep.

Fortunately, on that first day, as this realization washed over me, I was approached by my real driver, the transfer I'd arranged through my travel agency, the Mir Corporation, in the months prior to my trip. The driver and his girlfriend, who was along for the ride, plucked me from the crowd of freelance drivers and threw me and my sixty-pound hardback black Samsonite suitcase into his shiny Ford. Strange to see a brand-new American car in Eastern Europe. Stranger to see it driven by such a young man and his younger girlfriend with long shiny hair and polished fingernails. I began to wonder where the money for the car had come from. We drove along the tree-lined boulevards of Odessa on the way to the Chernoe More, the two of them quietly speaking Ukrainian or Russian—I wasn't sure which—between them.

As soon as I checked into the hotel (in reality, not four-star at all, but still $125 a night), I could almost hear the voices of my grandparents: "What are you doing there? We worked so hard to get our people out of there, and now you're spending money to return?" In the next few days, I would hear this question from many Ukrainian people I met—*you have money to travel, and you choose to come here?*

Each night, in my air-condition-less hotel room in a seemingly air-condition-less city, I tried unsuccessfully to sleep. No air could flow through the locked door, which I would have liked to prop open, but kept bolted out of safety concerns. In the middle of my first night just as I'd fallen asleep, I had gotten an odd phone call. When I picked up after the third ring, the man on the other end asked, "Is Olga there?"

"No," I said, "there's no one by that name here."

"Oh," he said, "she was there last night." Then after some hesitation, he added, "She is my wife," which struck me as such a blatant lie that it shocked me into realizing that he had been speaking English to me the entire time. Why had he known to speak English to me?

"No Olga here," I shouted and threw the receiver into the cradle. Then I went to my suitcase and got out the heavy bicycle u-clamp that I had packed to secure my suitcase while traveling on the Trans-Siberian railroad. I clutched the u-clamp in my palm under my pillow all night, but hardly slept a minute.

The next morning when Pavel arrived at the hotel, I told him the story. "Oh," he said, "you must be careful. There is organized crime here. They might call and offer you prostitutes." Then I remembered the husky and ruggedly handsome well-dressed body-builder types in sunglasses whom I'd seen hanging around the lobby of the Chernoe More when I'd checked in.

"I wouldn't worry though," Pavel added. "Organized crime owns the hotels and trains—the whole tourism industry. You're a tourist, so they won't target you." But, if I were an American businessman, he explained, I might have some cause for concern. None of this helped me sleep during my week in Odessa.

The object of this trip had been to gather a story about the ancestors who had come before me, and to find out what had become of the people from my ethnic group, the people my great-grandparents had left behind in Russia. As a practiced traveler, I was supposed to move through this place lightly or invisibly, like a neutral researcher or journalist.

But there's this problem that you have to take your body with you when you travel, which requires you to lug along clothing and shoes and books which weigh you down. The body that houses the eyes, the ears, the nose, the instruments for data retrieval has to come along, and it has needs. It has to eat, to breathe, to use bathrooms. All these things take time and money and draw your attention away from the story you're trying to find. And in an extreme situation, such as 120°F weather, these considerations multiply exponentially. You can't think of anything else. They become the story.

I remembered that earlier in the first half of my trip, while I was in Strasbourg, France, I rented a car and drove north to all the small Alsatian villages that had been listed by my ancestors as their villages of origin when they immigrated to Russia—Haguenau, Niederlauterbach, Wissenbourg. In one of these small villages, I found the Catholic church open, and I went inside the cool dark interior to sit in a pew for a few moments and offer a prayer asking for safety on the second half of my journey into

Eastern Europe. I was already beginning to feel anxiety about the ambition of my plan, concern that I had overextended myself.

Sitting there in that Alsatian church, I began to have the feeling that one of my ancestors, perhaps a great-great-great-grandmother, had sat in that very church, perhaps in that very pew, almost two hundred years earlier, and had worried and prayed about the same journey east that she was planning with her family. She wouldn't have been able to talk to anyone but God about the journey. The families who elected to migrate to Russia did so secretly, planning for weeks, then leaving their homes under cover of darkness for the long trek to the Danube where they boarded one-way pontoon boats that carried them to the Black Sea.

I felt my ancestor's prayers and worry in that moment sitting in the small dark church in Alsace. And I felt her uncertainty—would she make it, would her family survive? And in my own voice, I was able to answer the question. Yes, something of her had survived. I had come this way, full circle, all the way from America as evidence that sometimes the hardest thing we dream survives, that something of ourselves goes on.

Sitting on the hot Yak-40 plane on the runway in Odessa, destined to crash even before we take off, I think of this moment of grace back in the Alsatian church just weeks before. I begin to cry harder. The Russian businessman rises from his seat, comes across the aisle to me.

"Are you unwell?" he asks. "Can I help you."

"No, no," I dab my nose, "I'm just tired and hot."

He returns to his seat, and I make an effort to cry more quietly, in stifled hiccoughs, tears streaming down cheeks, nose-blowing, muffled-sob crying.

I reach into my backpack for another tissue and feel the edges of my books. I have brought many pounds of research materials with me on the trip, mostly histories of the German-Russian people such as privately published books written by survivors of some part of this long, complicated narrative of my people.

My backpack is heavy with books with titles like *Fateful Danube Journey*, one man's published journal of the trip east across Europe from Alsace to Odessa in 1803; and *Secret Death-Defying Escape Finally Told*, a novel published by Wally Wolsky about his grandfather's escape from communist Russia; or *We Ate the Salt of Russia*, a narrative of a few women who survived forced labor camps in Siberia.

When I reach into my backpack, the book that I pull out is *The Last Bridge: Her Own True Story, Told by Elvera Ziebart Reuer* and written by Marjorie Knittel. It's the story of Elvera Reuer's 2,500-mile overland trek as a young girl between the wartime years of 1940 and 1949 from her village in the Glueckstal region near the Black Sea in Russia to Germany and eventually onto the *Queen Elizabeth* in Hamburg en route to America.

When I open the book, I notice the first chapter begins with a proverb from the Bible: "Trust in the Lord with all thine heart and lean not unto thine own understanding. In all thy ways acknowledge Him, and He shall direct thy paths."

I'm not a religious person, not at all. I like to think I'm spiritual, but even when I was a kid and forced to attend church, I never could suspend disbelief during that "suffered, died on the cross, rose again in three days" part of the Nicene Creed. But, at this moment, I mean to say that the proverb comforted me, the idea of trusting the path. Immediately upon reading it, I stop whimpering, I begin to breathe easier.

So I'm not on the path that I had imagined for myself when I planned this research trip, but I am on some kind of path. Although I feel shame and disappointment in myself that I don't have the wherewithal to tough out the heat, to get on those trains to Moscow and eventually Siberia and find a way to meet those people and get the story. On the plane, I promise myself that I will return and try again someday, that I will someday tell their story.

And at that moment, with that promise made to myself, the pilot walks through the aisles to check on the passengers. He is a tall and capable looking Slav with large hands who leans down to explain to the passengers that he and the co-pilot will soon start up the engines so cooler air will begin to flow through the vents. He is about six foot, five inches, with white-blond hair and deep-cut cheekbones. And at the sight of him, instantly I know we are not going to crash.

Refusing Nostalgia

The past is a foreign country: they do things differently there.
—L.P. Hartley

When I asked my grandma Geist about the village in South Russia where my grandfather had emigrated from (Grandpa was notoriously quiet so you had to address all questions to Grandma Geist), she would say, "Oh, we all came from the same place." Hardly the stuff of legends.

I wanted the story of flight—the village he had left as a young boy under cover of darkness, the stale bread passed between many hands, the stony fields traversed in the middle of the night. I wanted the story of arrival—the storm-filled ocean passage, the train ride slicing across the North American continent, the first sight of the muddy streets of Eureka, the trading-post town in the Dakota Territory where our people purchased carts and oxen to transport themselves to their remote land claims yet farther in the north.

Instead, at gatherings where my grandparents would sit around and play cards with other couples they had known since youth, my grandmother might tell a joke in English, and then turn to Grandpa and say the punch line to him, in German. All the old people would laugh and rock in their seats. When I protested—for I didn't know German, we were encouraged to learn only English—my grandmother would insist that it was only funny in German. "There's no way to say it in English," she would explain.

Cultural amnesia—some small detour of meaning had occurred, something lost between the tongue and the brain. Even then, I felt myself cut loose on the ice floe of English—all the fun and forbidden stuff was happening in that other language they spoke. But now that they are all long gone, I realize that it was they who were drifting away on the ice floe of German. Now I am left behind, a fully vested American stranded without them on the mainland of English.

They made homes for themselves in the villages they created in South Russia in 1803, surviving the trauma of flight and exile from their original homeland in Western Europe, and they lived in those villages near the Black Sea as an ethnic minority for almost three generations. The promises they were given by the Czar—freedom from taxation, freedom from military service, the freedom to keep their own language, religions, and schools—held for about eighty years.

When some of those promises were withdrawn and young men from the villages were forcibly conscripted, my great-grandparents and their young children fled Russia and immigrated to America between the years 1886 and 1911. Answering the invitation for free land through the Homestead Act, they repeated the pattern of flight, exile, and resettlement in the Dakota Territory. This ethnic group, now sprinkled through much of the central United States, is called the Germans-from-Russia, a name that's fuzzy in its definitions and forever shaped by flux. The migrations that mark my ethnic group are preserved in their hyphenations, but the fact of their arrival in America was never codified in language. We never became the "German-from-Russia Americans," for example. Some stories are too long and complicated.

As a young girl, growing up in the 1950s and '60s in North Dakota, I was only vaguely aware of this ethnic history, but even the whiff of trauma and uprootedness was glamorous, especially against the everyday sameness of our hemmed-in farming enclave. Although Napoleon was a small midwestern town, it often felt eerily like an eighteenth-century European village that just happened to have televisions and automobiles. My grandfather made sausage and rhubarb wine in the basement. In the root cellar were rows of gleaming jars full of pickles and beets. Chores had to be done, and animals needed tending. My father's idea of a family outing was to pile all of us in the car on Sunday evenings and drive us around to look at the crops.

In this village of my hometown, rotund old men sat around on park benches gossiping with each other in German, and whiskery grandmothers endlessly baked and canned and sewed and gardened. There was a lot of church-going and polka-dancing. The older people spoke an archaic dialect of German, mixed with a broken English. In the local cafés, along with roast beef dinners or hamburgers and French fries on the menus were choices like knoephla soup, sauerkraut, and fleischkuekle.

They had little of the backward glance in them, my maternal grandparents. I would go so far as to say they refused nostalgia. The word "nostalgia" has its origins in Greek words, but not in Greek culture. Cobbled together from two Greek roots—*nostos* (meaning "return" or sometimes "journey") and *algeo* (meaning "pain," "sickness," or "sorrowful"), the term "nostalgia" was coined in 1688 by the Swiss Doctor, Johannes Hofer, to describe the "sad mood originating from the desire to return to native land." In *The Future of Nostalgia*, Svetlana Boym reports that Hofer first documented this phenomenon in various people displaced in the seventeenth century—"freedom loving students from the Republic of Berne studying in Basel, domestic help and servants working in France and Germany, and Swiss soldiers fighting abroad." Dr. Hofer observed that this new illness caused the afflicted to lose touch with the present, resulting in the "longing for the native land to become their single-minded obsession." The patients' symptoms included a "lifeless and haggard countenance," an "indifference toward everything," and "a confusion between past and present, real and imaginary events."[15]

According to Boym, Swiss scientists found that the simplest sensual cues of home, such as the tune of folk melodies of Alpine valleys, were likely to trigger a "debilitating nostalgic reaction in Swiss soldiers." Military superiors were forced to prohibit the soldiers from playing, singing, or even whistling native tunes. Later cures for bouts of nostalgia were more radical. Boym reports that in 1733 when the Russian army was striken by nostalgia just as it ventured into Germany, the commanding officers announced that the "first to fall sick [with nostalgia] would be buried alive," a practice which seemed to have an immediate palliative effect on the sufferer.[16]

In the case of all my great-grandparents and my two grandfathers, both of whom immigrated to the United States as young boys, I could theorize that the hardship of emigration and the privation they experienced after arrival was enough to shake the nostalgic impulse right out of them. But that remains a theory, because I have no records about the quality of their lives—no letter collections, no journals, no family stories. In the absence of information and into that negative space, it's difficult to formulate a theory. Perhaps the silence speaks for itself.

---

[15] Svetlana Boym, *The Future of Nostalgia* (Basic Books, 2001), pp. 3.
[16] Boym, p. 5.

When I go to the state archives for historical information about the early days of European settlement, I find that archival records do exist. Primary among them are the 1930s Works Progress Administration (WPA) records that employed writers to travel around counties in North Dakota and interview the remaining immigrant generation. A WPA interview form was utilized that asked general questions about family data (names/birthdates), date and year of passage, name of ship, cost of ticket, etc. A general prompt at the end of the interview form invited the interviewee to provide supplemental information in various categories such as "political events" (county seat fights, party caucuses, vigilanties), "social events" (weddings, dances, games), "industries" (trapping, soap making, picking buffalo bones), as well as a "miscellaneous" category that included "frost, hail, drought, cyclones, hoppers, blizzards, prairie fires, epidemics, Indian scares, claim jumpers, and etc."

The extensiveness and specificity of this final category leads one to assume there was a great deal of miscellaneous trouble to be found in the early days of the region. But what's even more striking about the WPA interview documents is the fact that while the interviews with Irish, English, German, Norwegian, and Swedish immigrants are often full of lively detail, the interviews with the German Russian immigrants tend to be shorter and filled with cursory details. One WPA worker jots a field observation at the end of a report: "I can get very little information from this couple. When I ask them what they do in their leisure time, they reply they have no leisure time . . . I can only assume they believe me to be an insurance salesman."[17]

All the WPA interviewees were invited to include a supplemental narrative, relaying additional anecdotes about early pioneer life. These were appended to the back of the formal WPA interview report. Perhaps it goes without saying that most of the

---

[17] WPA Interview Archives, 1939.

German-Russian interviews do not include additional material. By contrast, one loquacious interviewee, Peter Borr, who lists Michigan, Holland, and The Netherlands as the origin points of his family's multiple migrations, also includes a forty-eight page "Pioneer History," with subject headings as various as the "History of the Van Raalte Reformed Church," "Our Married Life," "Our Post Immigration Condition," "Home Construction in the Early Days," "Our Financial Experiences: The Ups and Downs," a "Political Horoscope from 1876," and a poem authored by Mr. Borr himself.

The most stunning section of the document, however, features an eight-page report titled, "North Dakota Sudden Deaths," in which Mr. Borr has taken it upon himself to note the details of 207 sudden or unusual deaths, such as the following, all of which occurred in the region between the years of 1886 and 1936.

> 1886: John Robinson shot by Carlson near Apple Creek.
>
> 1888: Bollinger kills self out of fear of arrest for not paying debts.
>
> 1891: James Findley shoots wife, then self to death near Winchester.
>
> 1888: Grens frozen to death east of Mound City.
>
> 1896: Young man killed by lightning while cultivating corn near Gackle.
>
> 1889: C. Hanson shoots his head off near Hull.
>
> 1898: Mrs. Reynolds found dead in shallow pond, shortly after Mr. Reynolds was found shot through the heart, lying on a log at Omio.
>
> 1913: L. Tinholt mysteriously disappears at his opera house, while it burns.

1927: Son of Mitchell dragged to death by pony nine miles north of Herried.

1929: J.J. Fenelon shoots self at Pollock.

1929: Becthold shot dead at Mobridge.

1923: Three children freeze to death under sleigh as they returned from school in storm.

1918: Jack Bickle dies from Dr. Till's treatments.

1924: M. Bickle crushed under wagon at Artas.

1920: C. Vorlander shoots self on daughter's grave at Eureka.[18]

Just this sampling of the death entries, simply stated in one-line summaries, reveals the violence, hardship, and trauma of the early days. Although my great-grandparents were immigrants and my grandparents were children and young adults during these years, none of these stories were told or remembered by the time I was growing up near or around the very place where these tragedies occurred. In fact, you wouldn't have had a clue (as I did not) that the older people of these towns had known and lived through harsh times. As I read these reports, I understand that they were engaged in a profound and willful act of silencing, an immaculate execution of cultural amnesia.

Instead of dwelling on the dead and the past, it seems they turned their attentions forward to us, their grandchildren, and outward, to the land itself. "Never let the land go out of the family." This is a caution I heard often and always growing up. As the owners of the center farm, the original homestead, my family has become the caretaker of a legacy that's important, if only conceptually, to cousins and uncles and aunts who live in places far and wide.

---

[18] Peter Borr, "Accidental and Sudden Deaths," Supplementary Report, Emmons County, WPA Interview Archives, 6 November 1939.

But what makes a piece of land go solid under your feet? How to explain this nostalgia for land that overtakes otherwise pragmatic people? "Settlement in a new, unknown, uncultivated country is equivalent to an act of Creation," Mircea Eliade observed in *The Myth of the Eternal Return*.[19] Wilderness or uncultivated regions, to the mind of immigrants, were part of the undifferentiated void, something that called out to be shaped and molded to our needs.

Eliade theorizes that when our ancestors performed rites of cultivation such as plowing, seeding, and finally inhabiting a piece of land, they saw themselves as "cosmicizing" it and making it sacred by matching its physical shape to the cosmic model or ideal that existed, if only in their imaginations. Like God, they were doing elemental things—separating the light from the dark, the earth from the sky, the land from the ocean. They were making order from chaos.

At that moment, according to Eliade, no matter how difficult the work, they felt their lives take on a greater resonance. Their actions connected them to ancient, ongoing patterns—what Eliade described as a "ceaseless repetition of gestures"—and through these gestures they felt their connection to a chain of being that stretched back far beyond themselves to known and unknown ancestors.[20]

Family land, by association, becomes the locus, the site that records the sacrifices and successes of our ancestors. All the details of the people and the hardships become conflated across centuries, folded in, tucked away and eventually forgotten by succeeding generations. After that general forgetting is complete, only the *fact* of the land remains, a geographical reminder connecting us to all those who came before.

---

[19] Mircea Eliade, *The Myth of the Eternal Return: Or, Cosmos and History* (Princeton University Press, 1954), p. 10.
[20] Eliade, p. 5.

This fusion of home and land in the minds of those who re-main is often expressed in Willa Cather's *O Pioneers!* People are fleeting and ephemeral, she observes, but the land holds the future. "How many of the names on the county clerk's plat will be there in fifty years?" Cather writes. "We come and go, but the land is always here. And the people who love it and understand it, are the people who own it—for a little while."[21]

Whatever sentimentality I may have observed in my grand-parents about land or people may be more accurately defined as *heimat*, a German concept that's equally as complex as nostalgia, but even more problematic. *Heimat* can mean an attachment to homeland, abode, landscape, or habitat. But its meaning is also elusive and has been reinterpreted for political ends, especially to justify excluding populations deemed by the majority not to "belong" to a particular landscape.

At its core, Felipe Hernandez explains in *Transculturation*, the concept of *heimat* describes a sense of integrity or whole-ness in a place, "a feeling of belonging together in one place, a feeling of being at home." But it's also an illusion. "*Heimat* is such that if one would go closer and closer to it, one would dis-cover that at the moment of arrival it is gone. It has dissolved into nothingness."[22]

And so as I try to approach describing it, the ache for that place I was born to and these people I was bound to—whole gen-erational waves of family members who have disappeared from my view—the ache only increases even as the image fades. And so I realize that I am the one who suffers most acutely from nos-talgia, not only from the loss of that feeling of belonging or *hei-mat* that they created for me as a child, but also from regret that the illusion of home they presented felt so solid and claustropho-

[21] Willa Cather, *O Pioneers!* (Book-of-the-Month-Club, 1996), p. 308.
[22] Helen Thomas, "Colonizing the Land: Heimat and the Constructed Landscapes of Mex-ico's Ciudad Universitaria," Felipe Hernandez, editor, *Transculturation* (Leiden, Nether-lands: Brill, 2008), p. 110.

bic to me as a child that all I could do was bristle against it, then engineer my escape, sealing my separation from the people and place that now as an adult I am compelled to haunt in my imagination, returning again and again.

Perhaps this is just the natural condition of aging and loss. My grandparents had the doubly-complex dilemma of having a past that was not only figuratively a foreign country—the natural foreign country that all childhoods are when we glance back at them from the far distance of our later years—but also a past that was literally a foreign country, one about which they did not seem to have memory or language to share with us. And so I experience nostalgia for them in multiple layers—ache for my own foreign country of childhood and ache for all the foreign countries of their unique history that disappeared unarticulated on my grandparents' foreign tongues.

Now I spend my time searching through old newspapers, written in languages I do not know, through letter collections and archives in quiet library aisles. I visit graveyards, nursing homes. I smile at old people I see in the street, hoping they will tell me something about the old days. I have an obsessive habit of scanning the faces of modern-day refugees I see in news reports on CNN, hoping to get a glimpse of the familiar, a long lost grandparent.

Most of the time it's sad and lonely work, this reclamation of the past, and then sometimes you get lucky. A few years ago, when I was doing research for *The Horizontal World: Growing Up Wild in the Middle of Nowhere*, my memoir about growing up a rebellious farmer's daughter on a North Dakota wheat farm, I visited older relatives and asked them questions about the old days. Usually my questions were met with the same silences and suspicions that the WPA workers likely faced when they traveled around for the interview project in the 1930s.

Then one day, during a very ordinary conversation at my older cousin Tony's kitchen table, he began to tell me about the milk letters he remembered that had come for my great-grandfather from the brothers and sisters he had left behind in the Black Sea villages when they fled.

Tony was only a boy at the time, but he remembered that the letters from Russia were written in two layers, the first of which was visible to the eye, penned in ink or pencil, reporting mundane news from the village (births, natural deaths, weddings). Well into the 1920s, my great-grandfather received these letters from his brothers and sisters he had left behind in Russia. By then, he was a prosperous North Dakota landowner, but the news from Russia only grew more troubling.

The second layer of the letter, Tony said—invisible and written in milk between the ink lines—was blown dry on the breath of the worried author to make it undetectable to the eyes of the government censor. This second layer, the milk letter, recounted the horrors of life under Communism. It begged for money and detailed reports of mass starvation and farm collectivization in my great-grandfather's home village. The milk letter told of grave robbing, church stripping, and of sons and fathers herded up and taken either to servitude in the Russian military or to forced labor camps in Siberia.

My cousin Tony remembers my great-grandfather sitting on a stool in front of the north window of our farmhouse, tears streaming down his otherwise stoic face, as he held the shaking letter up to the sunlight to illuminate the lines written in milk. A few years later, Tony recalls, in the early 1930s, the letters stopped coming and all talk of Russia ceased.

I grew up in that farmhouse in the 1960s. I sat at that north window, most often scanning the highway for the bus or the carload of friends that was coming to take me for some adventure in town. One road led to another, all of them away. But I'm ready now to take up my spot at that window, to hold everything up to the fiercest light, to report the invisible layers of stories I find hidden there.

Not All There

A few years ago, my friend Jordan, who is a writer and park ranger in northern California, decided to take a month-long trip to Teton National Park to do some research for a book. He had worked for the park service twenty years earlier in the Tetons, so the trip was part research, part reverie, and part mournful return to the rougher mountains of his youth. He was one of those people who competed in and won biathlons—the Olympic winter sport where you ski, then shoot with a rifle, then ski some more. He liked to claim you could drop him into any unfamiliar terrain with a compass and a knife—maybe not even a knife—and expect that he'd survive as long as needed.

His whole take on the world was strange and unfamiliar to me. As a born and bred flatlander, a midwesterner, and someone who grew up in tame farm country, not even as wild as the ranch country that existed west of the 100th meridian, I feel unsafe as soon as my car encounters the inclines of foothills. I never grew up around water, so I can't swim and am deathly afraid of water. I was never big on hiking or backpacking or camping. One time when I was around eight, I slept outside with my sisters in a makeshift tarp-tent on the far edge of our very big back farmyard, and I woke up the next morning with an earache.

As a fuzzy, red infection grew in my ear canal over the next few days and my parents hemmed and hawed about the doctor (we, none of us, ever liked going to the doctor—doctors were for when you were taken out flat on a stretcher), my parents finally took me to the doctor and discovered that a bug had crawled into my ear overnight and died.

Probably, the night we were camping, Dr. Goodman reasoned, as he held it up between the tips of his tiny forceps for us all to see. That was it for me—no more sleeping outside. Bugs crawl in your ear and die when you go camping!

How Jordan and I ever became friends is a mystery. But, in anticipation of his Teton trip, I bought him a *Wyoming Atlas and Gazetteer* as a kind of joke, because orienteering is one of his most prized skills. Before I slipped the atlas in the manila envelope to ship off to him in California, I flipped through the pages to see what could possibly make people speak in such reverential tones about Grand Teton National Park.

When I opened the section that focused on the north-south corridor of the Rockies containing the Tetons, I was surprised to discover that practically every glaciated range, every horn, cirque, moraine, wrinkle, valley, and rubble pile that the alpine glaciers left behind in northwest Wyoming had been named, and, in fact, bore some of the grandest names in American history—Roosevelt, Jackson, Bridger.

At the time, I was working on a memoir about growing up a rebellious farmer's daughter on a North Dakota wheat farm. One of my working premises was that the place where I grew up was a no-place in the national imagination. One ethnographer dubbed the five-county area in central North Dakota where I grew up the "sauerkraut triangle," because it was so heavily populated with people from my ethnic group, known as Germans-from-Russia, and, presumably, if you drifted into this region as a hapless traveler, you might fall under the spell of sauerkraut's vinegary ethers and never find your way back to the interstate again.

The Wyoming Gazetteer inspired me. If some of the country's most unpopulated and inaccessible peaks were so lovingly named—geological nuance after geological nuance—what might the DeLorme Gazetteer have to say about the milder nooks and crannies of my own home ground, a lightly populated region, but certainly inhabited and well used.

Not surprisingly, Barnes & Noble did not have a copy of the North Dakota Gazetteer, so I ordered it from Amazon, and waited for days, anticipating its arrival, imagining all the delicious place names that people before me had coined for the topo map of my childhood.

Perhaps you already know what happened when the package came, when I ripped it from its wrapper and turned to the pages containing my hometown, my county, the township of my family land.

I found only the few names I already knew—Napoleon (town), Logan (county), Bryant (township). Highway 3, the two-lane blacktop that I used to gaze at from my bedroom window and dream about escaping on, was also there.

The rest of the map was colored in with greens, browns, and tans blocking out the geographical relief of the land, the collection of concentric circles indicating small hills, black lines for roads, thin blue lines for streams. But there were few place names on the paper, nothing trekked and traced by feet and fingers of love, mapping the curvilinear geography. The pages were full of green expanses, blank and silent about themselves.

I knew from my childhood that people had lived there, worked, walked, died there. Everything imaginable and unimaginable had happened on this small piece of land, but the places must not have struck people as name-worthy—not enough to garner the attention of the DeLorme geographers anyway.

Not all there is a phrase that people in my hometown might use to describe someone who was "slow" or "developmentally disabled," as we like to say now.

In my hometown, there was a man named Rochus who walked the same route through town each day, no matter what the weather—up the main street from his mother's house where he lived, through the grain elevators, past the café, grocery store, and bar. And when he went by the Stock Grower's Bank, he would shout "big shot, big shot," at the top of his lungs. Every day. And sometimes if we kids came into his path, he'd stop and smile at us, as if he was just a very big kid in overalls himself, and he'd point his finger at us and yell, "How much, how much? Two cents? Sold!"

All this was terrifying and inexplicable to us as kids, but it was explained away to us by the adults as nothing to worry about, because Rochus was "not all there."

It's okay, we might say to ourselves about the unnamed state of the Midwest, *we're just not all there*. The streets you drive, the places where you slept, the willows and sycamores under which you wept and fell in love—not all there. The haunted places of my youth, like the alley of raspberry bushes on the way to my grandmother's house or the dip in the moraine east of my hometown where we used to have keg parties—just blank creases in topographical maps until someone takes the time to remember, to bring a word, then a phrase and sentence to them. To remember is to *re-member*, after all, as in reattach something like a lost limb, to bring story back to an unstoried landscape.

I'm willing to fight about this. I'm willing to stand up and come to fisticuffs in bars about this, drink a Budweiser even, surrounded by jars of turkey gizzards and billiard tables, insisting that the Midwest is not a no-place. Not in the way that Gertrude Stein meant it about her own hometown, Oakland, California, when she said, "There's no there there." Despite what the world of maps, letters, and history doesn't say about the Midwest, there is *plenty* of there there.

More accurately, I think we are a "true" place, in the way that Herman Melville meant it when he wrote, "It's not down in a map. True places never are." So, no more *aw-shucks*-ing about the place where we live. No more digging our toe in the dirt. From now on, let's just declare the Midwest a true place full of open secrets, most of them delicious and horrifying. We have such a backlog of work to do! Whole centuries of odd facts and bizarre occurrences to record about what's really been going on here, the details of which we must now regretfully disclose to the rest of the known world.

Postcards from Boomtown

In 2008, the U.S. Geological Survey sparked a fracking boom in North Dakota when they announced that 3 to 4.3 billion barrels of recoverable oil rested under the state in the Bakken/ Three Forks formation. Estimates of additional oil reserves that are not recoverable with current technology are between 18–24 billion barrels. At present, over one million barrels a day are extracted from the Bakken shale.

1.

Things go boom in the Bakken. Daily. A minivan burns to cinders in the Williston Walmart parking lot—someone's living room/ bedroom/kitchen, someone's illegal and unwisely used propane heater. Temperatures hover at -15°F and people are living in small throwaway RVs held together by duct tape. Nowhere to put all the people, and the arsonists aren't helping.

A half-built apartment complex in Minot burns down one week. And the next week, another half-built apartment complex burns down in Williston. Workers and even sometimes families live in man camps, military rows of paper-thin aluminum storage pods the size of jail cells—a bed, a sink, a five-step walking space, a chair in the corner.

Meanwhile, back at Walmart, explosions of other kinds. A few years ago, Walmart made the decision to just put merchandise out in pallets. Mountains of women's pants and blouses, scattered piles of toys, bundles of Carhartt jackets, steel-toed boots balanced against walls, thrown in corners. The pallets empty and fill, empty and fill. In the early years of the boom, no one to hang things up, straighten, sort, put out displays. Walmart can't keep employees, and the goods keep coming along with people sifting through piles looking for things they need, things to buy.

The post office can't keep employees because rent is too high and roads are too dangerous. In December of 2014, six postal workers in Williston walked off the job in one day. No one knows where anyone lives anyway—forwarding addresses are only rumors. (Later, a discovery that postal workers were simply throwing mail away in dumpsters, to dispose of undeliverable mail.)

Even murders start as rumors. Last week the police announced they were investigating a murder. They had no crime scene, no body. Just the rumor of a murder, so they asked the public to keep an eye out. Sure enough, a day later a body turned up under a bloody mattress in the ditch 13 miles east of Williston. Welcome to Boomtown.

And the roads are dangerous, not only for little postal worker vehicles creeping along the shoulders. In one location on Highway 85 just south of Williston (a town of about 14,000), a traffic count was conducted a few years ago. In one 24-hour period, 29,000 vehicles went through the intersection—60 percent of which were semitrailer trucks.

To run to the grocery store in your Civic Honda because you forgot to buy beans for your chili is to take your life into your hands. You must make careful lists. You must try not to forget anything. Because things go boom in the Bakken. Daily.

The oil has been down there for millions of years, a worker named Sven tells me, *but suddenly we are in such a hurry.*

2.

A Facebook page titled, "Bakken Oilfield Fail of the Day," records daily mishaps. Pictures of oil spurting in the air or recovered fracking water—known as flowback water—on fire, shooting out of a rig. Pictures of overturned semis, water tankers, belly dump trucks in ditches.

Any photo of a vehicle on its side in the ditch will cause someone on the FB page to write, "sleepy, had to take a nap" or "that'll buff right out." A Caterpillar being loaded off a platform slips a wheel on the ramp and falls on its side. Under the picture, someone's written, "Musta been a woman driver."

Women drivers and southern drivers are a big topic of discussion in the Bakken, as are wind and weather. A picture of a trailer home, blown onto its side, has the caption, "Wind, 1, Trailer, 0."

Beside a photograph of several twenty-foot-tall water storage tanks blown over in a field like playthings, someone has written:

Do you know why North Dakota is so windy?
Because Montana blows and Minnesota sucks.

3.

Driving through the Bakken at night is like moving through an enemy encampment of biblical proportions; it's like seeing what Alexander the Great saw when cresting a hill and coming upon the thousand campfires of the Persian Army.

All around in the darkness are the pumping arms of oil rigs, or the tall, well-lit fracking towers, or refineries in the distance like small bright cities. Beside each oil pad is a four-to-five-foot plume of fire burning straight out of a pipe coming out of the ground.

This practice, known as flaring, has allowed oil companies to burn off 30 percent of the natural gas that comes up to the surface along with the shale oil they are extracting. No infrastructure yet exists in the region to collect the natural gas, and the practice of flaring—in addition to being wasteful—increases the amount of greenhouse gas emissions released into the atmosphere.

How much waste is this? At present, oil companies are extracting a million barrels of oil a day in the Bakken. And in one average month 9.4 billion cubic feet of natural gas will be flared off into the atmosphere. One blogger, Jim Fuglie, tried to do the math. He got out his Montana Dakota Utilities bill to see how many cubic feet of natural gas it took to heat his home during the coldest month of the year. The number was 12,000 cubic feet. By his calculations, the state could heat 780,000 homes a month with the natural gas that's been flared off.

Ironically, just this week, a woman in Fort Yates froze to death inside her home on the Standing Rock Indian Reservation because the tribe is facing a shortage of propane to heat homes.

The state legislators don't seem interested in slowing the boom by forcing infrastructure improvements to correct these imbalances, and none of these problems are going away. Conservative estimates are that there are between 20 to 40 billion barrels of extractable shale oil in the Bakken and Three Forks formation.

4.

The stories that involve children stay with you the longest. It's one thing to listen to John tell you about how he lost his job as a state archeologist because of budget cuts in Kansas and how he blew through their savings, just trying to maintain some sense of normalcy for their daughter, who is now nine. They kept thinking something was bound to come through for John, and then his wife, Ellen, lost her job, too, and now their retirement money is gone.

And it's hard enough to listen with averted eyes and murmur something about the "downturn of the economy," which causes John to actually sneer at you a bit even as he hears it, because Ellen was the one who finally got the job teaching in Williston (because they can't keep teachers in Boomtown either, so there's always a job for someone desperate enough to move there).

And now John and Ellen live in a small RV because rent for a two-bedroom apartment is somewhere around $3,000 and John has to bunk over at his buddy's trailer at night, so that Ellen and their daughter can have a little privacy.

5.

Everyone on the Bakken has a story about children, it seems, and usually they are stories of separation—children being raised in Texas, in Montana, in Wyoming by someone else.

"Every time I talk to her she says 'Daddy, when you coming home,'" one wildcatter tells me one night sitting by the fireplace in the lobby of the hotel (he's just come from the strip club and is very drunk).

He's already told me how much he makes an hour ($48/hour = $164,000 year with overtime), and how much he lost tonight at blackjack ($500). We've talked about his mother, his ex-wife, his wife, and his girlfriend, and now we are on the subject of his daughter. "She misses me, sure," he says, "but she's going to have a great Christmas."

The next day, another woman tells me a story about one night when she was working as a waitress, and a man came into the restaurant with his two little kids. They were maybe eight and ten. The man was still in his muddy work clothes. It was late, she said—about 11 p.m., but he had toys for them. They sat together quietly in a booth and played and colored on the placemats. When the waitress took their order, she smelled alcohol on the man, really strong. She went back in the kitchen and tried to decide what to do. Should she call the police?

Stay out of it, the older waitress advised.

"No," the girl said, "if something happens to those kids, I won't forgive myself."

So she pulled the man aside and said, "I smell alcohol on you and I'm not going to let you leave the restaurant with those kids. Give me your keys."

I'm not giving you my keys, the man said.

Well, then I'm calling the cops, she responded.

He said, don't do that. I drive for a living. I can't lose my license. Then he begins to tell her how his wife left him and he has no one to take care of the kids. He just picked them up from daycare. I can't lose my job, he says.

So she told me she ran back to the kitchen and thought, "What would Mom do?"

Then she struck on this idea to let the man go ahead in his car, and she'd follow behind in her car with the kids. He agreed to this. When they got to the man camp, the guy came over to her car to gather his kids, and he said, "Thank you. No one's ever done something like that for me. I promise this won't happen again." But the waitress told me she doubts it.

"I just wish they would never have found that oil," she said to me. "I just wish they'd go get oil somewhere else."

I tell her how this oil has changed the national economy. Politicians are saying it's lessening our dependence on oil-rich rogue nations—all those places we've been going to fight wars for the last few decades.

"They call it 'conflict-free' oil," I tell her.

"It doesn't feel conflict-free to me," she says.

The Death of a Lost Dog

I'm going to tell you what happened to Musa up front, so that you don't get too attached to him like I did over the two weeks that so many of us got swept up in the search for him. I'm telling you the ending first not to make you sadder, but because I think there's something else worth saying here, something beyond the story of the death of a lost dog.

First off, people are good. Or maybe it's that dog people are especially good. During the short period of Musa's freewheeling, I learned that people were willing to spend their nights and weekends walking the fields calling his name. They kept an eye out, reported sightings, checked back, then inquired about our progress.

I was living at the time in a multiplex on the southwest side of Ames on a cul-de-sac called Pinon Drive that overlooks College Creek, which runs east-west through the city. One Saturday in October, I looked out the second-floor window of my office and saw this small dog standing beside the garbage dumpster. No collar, no leash, no owner calling his name from a distance—just a little brownish-black dog with long ears looking around, trying to get his bearings.

Maybe it was that hesitation in his stance, his blinking glance toward the parking lot, as if searching for a familiar car, that made me determined to bring him inside. It was a Dachshund, I could see from the short legs, extended torso, and pointed snout.

College Creek, including the muddy shore and the trees and brush that contours it, serves as a natural corridor inside the city for all kinds of wild things. At least eight or nine rabbits make permanent residence there, as do owls and red-tailed hawks. From my balcony, it wasn't unusual to see a dozen deer grazing in the adjacent field or to spy a coyote or fox or pot-bellied opossum (although never at the same time), moving under the whispery canopy.

The industrial-sized dumpster that the Dachshund now stood beside was backed up into the trees, which made it a way station for migrating animals, mostly because of the three raccoons who serviced the dumpster nightly by fishing out garbage. While all else slept, the raccoons wrestled bags to the ground and inventoried their contents on the ground.

The college students who lived in the nearby multiplexes weren't the most fastidious about consolidating leftovers, so often in the morning when I took my dogs out for their first walk, I'd find cheeseburger and French fry remnants splayed out in their greasy wrappers, or eviscerated Styrofoam containers with yellow curry or beans and rice littering the ground. A staff member from the complex came around daily to clean up the area, but the grease and food droppings, crushed into the dirt, must have broadcast the site to hungry critters.

The windows of my writing desk overlooked this dumpster. I didn't monitor the goings-on. Let's just say that my dog Buttons, a Bichon-Lhasa mix, kept me apprised of events on the ground from the armchair by the window where he posted himself, keeping the garbage safe for the neighborhood.

In the eight years since I'd adopted him and his litter mate, Benjamin, I had learned to read their dog signs: growls and low ruffs meant people were on the move (how dare our neighbors go outside and start their cars); barking meant someone was walking a dog; frantic barking meant that a dented, blue van was parked outside and the couple that drove it had climbed into the dumpster for more efficient gleaning.

Uncanny stillness or whining and incessant staring usually meant that Buttons detected the proximity of wild animals. Benjamin, his brother, who went blind from cataracts at age five, usually sat beside Buttons and looked unseeingly out the window, amplifying Buttons's cues by barking louder than you can imagine a fluffy twenty-pound dog could bark. This uproar must have been what caused me to look outside and spy Musa for the first time.

Several times since I adopted Benjamin and Buttons, I have seen unattended dogs on the street and I've always turned around to get them under my control. I pursued two Pomeranians across a soybean field in flip-flops. I led a food-motivated black Lab down the street with treats until we found his house. I corralled two ebullient Huskies until the owner could be located. If it were my dogs, I would want someone to do the same for me.

So, when I saw the Dachshund, I grabbed a bag of treats and a dog leash and headed downstairs. The dog lifted his head when he heard me. He seemed to step toward me, then swiveled and ducked behind the dumpster. Along the tree line, I ran and called after him, *hey, buddy*, but I was not his buddy. This is how I learned that Dachshunds can really run, despite their cartoonishly short legs.

Once upstairs, I posted a notice on "Ames People," which is the place on Facebook to go when you want to find out what's going on in Ames, Iowa. It has about 25,000 members. Although it's moderated, it can be a quarrelsome group if you dare to post your unvarnished political opinions. But if the cable or power goes out, if there's odd weather threatening, if there are unexpected sirens in the middle of the night, or if there's mysterious construction downtown, all you need to do is check in with Ames People and someone will give you the whole story.

"Has anyone lost a Dachshund?" I posted, along with general whereabouts and a stock photo, because the dog was so fast that I couldn't snap an actual picture.

Within minutes, I was in contact with his pet sitter, whose clutches he had escaped. The dog's name was Musa, an unneutered male who had left behind his breeding mate and a two-pup litter. His owner was out of the country for the next few weeks, so the pet sitter was frantic to recover Musa.

Soon sightings poured in. "Saw this dog on the sidewalk heading south on South Dakota this morning." The pet sitter lived on Coconino, a few streets south of me across Mortensen, a main thoroughfare. So Musa must have crossed to Pinon, a relatively pastoral area along the creek's edge that connected green space behind the middle school to the east, sloping lawns, walking paths, a public park, and a quiet expanse behind a hospice to the north. For urban living, a runaway dog could not have picked a finer spot.

I traversed these acres during the next two weeks shouting, "Musa! Musa!" While I did this, I met other people also calling *Musa, Musa*—one woman with her teenage daughter, another woman with a toddler, and another woman towing two leashed Dachshunds that she hoped would attract the runaway.

Days passed. People checked in: "Any sign of Musa?" From postings, I began to detect his daily pattern. He took his mornings in the public park up north then migrated south by mid-day on public sidewalks or walking paths. He likely slept along the creek where dug-in hovels and brambles provided cover, a conclusion I arrived at when I noticed that the local raccoons had ceased their nightly marauding.

Late in the afternoons, I started putting out expensive tuna toppers on a paper plate beside the dumpster. I'd wait nearby, but he would not emerge for the food until I went back inside.

One day, I saw a couple ducking under the tree line calling, "Musa." They were the parents of Musa's owner, who was still out of the country and was frantic with worry. Another day, I saw two women in a pickup circling the cul-de-sac calling, "Musa." They had driven in from Cambridge, sixteen miles away. "We saw the posts on Facebook," they said, "and we couldn't sit by and do nothing."

This is what I'm telling you: People can be so good.

When I was a kid growing up on a dairy farm in North Dakota, we always had a dozen barn cats and at least one dog, usually a German Shepherd-Collie mix with a light brown coat. All the animals lived outside and sheltered in the barns. This was a line my mother set down that no one crossed—bringing animals inside the house. Not even sick kittens or baby rabbits. The outside was for outside. The porch on the front of our house had a mud room where all the stinky boots, barn coats, and guns were left. The inside of our farmhouse was polished and neat as any house in town.

Some of our neighbors, we knew, brought ailing lambs and calves inside to nurse them through some crisis. But my mother saw this as an evolutionary step backward, returning to days when our European ancestors had lived in large-roofed structures compartmentalized so that the animals lived in the back and the humans lived in the front. I have since toured a posh renovated farmhouse in southern France with gourmet kitchens and original art hanging on walls that still retains the running trough along the floor by which the animals' excretions were once flushed outside. My mother was a modern fifties housewife. She pushed our clan toward all the benefits of modernity such as Melmac plates, hamburger hot dishes, and fancy Jell-o molds.

On the farm, we had a succession of four or five dogs, all called Tippy, because one of them—I suppose the first—had a dark brown tip on his tail. The dog spent its days on the front stoop rising to wag its tail or brush against us as we came and went.

One Tippy lost his life defending the perimeter of our farm against a rabid fox. Another Tippy or possibly two were hit by passing station wagons or school buses full of children. A re-placement Tippy always appeared. They were a fixture of the farm, eating our food scraps and drinking milk sloshed into a crusted bowl in the milk barn.

I don't recall ever asking my parents about their individual origins or fates. I think of this with shame, now that I live in a house with two dogs who communicate their preferences to me in impatient stares, aloof postures, fervent paw jabs, and compli-cated verbal cues. Buttons often appears on the verge of speaking. When he's around groups of conversing humans, he hinges his mouth open and shut, as if to mimic talking. Even he looks sur-prised when no words flow out.

I was tricked by literature into becoming a dog-person. One fall about eleven years ago, I had two students who were writing es-says about their dogs. One missed his show dog Tucker, a reg-istered Springer Spaniel, whom he'd regretted leaving behind in Ohio where he was sure his parents weren't caring for the dog properly. Another wrote about her rescue dog Flower, an un-known combination of Irish and Border Terrier along with Aus-tralian Shepherd traces. She wrote about meeting the truck that brought Flower from South Carolina to Maine where she lived. She wrote about the profound difference Flower had made in her life.

Between reading these essays, I would take breaks and go online to look at petfinder.com, a dangerous activity, which is also how I came to discover that a puppy mill in Fort Dodge had recently been raided by authorities in central Iowa. The animal hospital in Jewell, Iowa, had posted pictures of the dozens of adoptable Maltese, Shih Tzu, and Pomeranian puppies from the litters that had been seized during the raid.

Five months old at the time, Buttons and Benjamin were listed along with their sister, whom the shelter had named Tiffany. They are a hypo-allergenic Bichon-Lhasa mix sometimes referred to as La-Chons. In the photos, they looked a little pathetic, their hair overgrown and matted. The Jewell Animal Hospital was taking applications, but they stated it would take time to process the dogs, which included neutering some, updating shots, checking for things like heartworm and Bordetella, and grooming to make them more presentable.

One click online always leads to another click and then another. I suppose that's why they call it the web. Soon, I was learning about the travesty of puppy mills—the terrible conditions inside these facilities, the breeder dogs that produce litter after litter until they are worn out, then euthanized. The litters are kept in cages 24/7 with nothing but food thrown in for them to share. They are never handled or taken outside to run or play.

The cages are stacked on top of each other and unlined, so the dogs sleep on wire mesh and go to the bathroom where they stand. The excrement falls through the wire of the stacked cages until reaching the floor where presumably it's hosed off from time to time. The puppies grow like this in the cages until they can be sold away, often to pet stores.

I don't know if I was ever able to watch those ASPCA commercials where Sarah McLachlan sings "In the Arms of an Angel," while images scroll by of emaciated, rheumy-eyed dogs shivering behind fences in dirty sheds, but after reading about puppy mills, I found I could never make it through another one of these ads.

And that very day, without thinking, I filled out an adoption form for Tiffany, the Bichon-Lhasa mix—because she was a female and there was only one of her—but soon the shelter contacted me to let me know that Tiffany was already on her way to a home in Rhode Island.

"Would you be interested in the boys?" the people from the shelter wrote me, sending a link to a video of Buttons and Benjamin.

Deviously, the animal hospital had filmed the two male dogs together at their very moment of intake while the matted puppies were sniffing around the floor of the vet clinic like hoover vacuum cleaners. "Are they girls or boys?" one technician asks another.

"I think that one's a girl," one worker says, pointing the camera at Buttons just as he lifts his leg and pees on the base of the metal table.

"Awk," the technician says affectionately. "I guess they're both boys."

How could I possibly choose between them? Believe it or not, I watched this video endlessly and found it endearing, until I brought them home and installed them in my apartment, which was all carpeted, except for the kitchen and bathrooms which were tiled. Not knowing if the puppies were house broken, that first night, I sequestered them in the master bathroom and texted my partner, Tom, who lives in Michigan and wrote, "I am the stupidest person on earth."

As the days passed with multiple sightings of Musa, mid-October transitioned to late-October and the night temperatures edged down to 30°F. Each night, I'd walk the perimeter and call out his name, then I'd go to bed thinking about Musa—where was he sleeping, what was he eating?

I imagined him bone-thin, shivering in some muddy indentation along the creek. But the next time I would see him, he did not look reduced by his circumstances. He remained full-bodied with a shiny black coat, growing stronger and faster by the day.

Dachshunds are scent hounds that were bred for hunting badgers. Their name derives from the German *dachs*, which means "badger" and *hund*, which means "hound." In Europe, they are still used in packs for hunting wild boars, but they will also go after foxes and any tunneling animal like rabbits. Learning this, I began to worry about my backyard menagerie—the unwary squirrels I often watched rolling around in the grass, the silly rabbits I observed chasing and hopping over each other in play. There was a new enforcer in town. Our weird little ecotone where wild, domestic, and human had intersected in an unnatural balance was being recalibrated. I even felt sorry for the wily bandit raccoons.

Somewhere around the end of that first week, I had made "lost dog" posters with a Dachshund photo and hung them around the buildings with my phone number. I began getting calls from college dudes who were just sitting out on their balconies enjoying a beer on a sunny afternoon: "Saw Musa pass by a few minutes ago."

And by now, I had been in contact with Musa's owner who was preparing for the long flight back home. I was texting him updates and photos of Musa whenever I spied him by the dumpster. "He eats the food I set out, then runs away. The stinker!" I wrote. The owner offered little bits of information about Musa's history. The dog was beloved and celebrated in their family. One year, he wrote, they even declared it "The Year of the Musa, like it was some kind of Chinese festival or something."

As the days unfolded and more people joined the search, the owner wrote me, "This is such a weird story. Fat weiner dog lives by dumpster by the creek and the whole town feeds him." Another friend on Facebook agreed: "He is being a weiner fo' sure."

We felt certain that Musa would respond to his owner's voice. The day he returned home, the owner came over and walked the creek, but no dog appeared. We agreed that I would call him to come over as soon as I had another sighting. But when this happened later that day, it took some time for the owner to get there and Musa was long gone again.

"I think the main problem is that I told him I was going to have him neutered when I got back home," the owner joked. "I mean, I was trash-talking him right to his face after he peed on the table legs and laundry basket for the 150th time."

After I adopted my dogs, I started working on my mother to get a pet. She had since moved off the farm and lived in town with no animals around. My father had been gone for several years. Mom admitted a house cat might be a good companion, so she went to a nearby farm and picked out a cute little kitten which proceeded to bite her hands and claw the furniture, unroll the toilet paper, and jump into every basket and cardboard box. It was exhausting. After a few days, she took the kitten back to the farm.

"Wow, glad she wasn't able to return us when we got to be too much," one of my sisters commented.

Sometime later when I was visiting my mom, she came out of the bedroom one morning and said, "I had a dream that the doorbell rang, and when I opened the door, there were two orange cats standing on the front step waiting to come in." It was a sign. She suggested, "Let's go up to the shelter in Bismarck and see if we can find an older cat for me."

So, we did and that's how she got her majestic male cat, Von Trapp, who is an orange tabby with gold eyes that match his coat. Mom treats him like the royalty he is. He gets to hop up and even sit on the kitchen counter sometimes. ("She never let us do that when we were kids," the same sister said.) Von Trapp has a crystal goblet that he drinks from and a ready supply of treats. He's not the svelte prince he once was. He's spreading around the middle, a result of living in a house with too much love.

And that's what pets do for us. They allow us to give away all of the unused love that's clogging our hearts, and it opens up the valves so that more love can flow through. Because love doesn't subtract, it multiplies.

Now whenever Mom and I talk on the phone, we begin by telling each other what our pets have been doing. One day, when I marveled how I had never paid attention to our farm dogs, she tells me this story about our last Tippy.

When they sold the farm to my brother, Rick, they decided that Tippy would stay on the land with Rick, who had a young family. An old dog had no place at the new house in town. On the farm, he'd have kids to play with, and he'd be at home in the familiar.

But the day after my parents moved, Rick called to report that Tippy had gone missing. They waited for days, but the dog didn't return home. A few days later they learned that Tippy had been shot by a farmer who lived several miles away, near some northerly land that my parents also farmed.

"Whenever we left with the pickup," my mother said, "he would wait to see if we turned north or south at the highway." If the pickup turned south that meant that they were going to town and Tippy would settle in for a nap. But if they turned north, Tippy would head out for the northerly acres. Because he was traveling across the fields, he'd always get there first. Tippy would be waiting for them up north when they arrived in the pickup.

"I never thought about how much he relied on us," my mom said. "He must have wondered why we didn't come home, so he went looking for us." We sat in silence for a minute, thinking about obedient Tippy running the miles of fields near the northerly acres searching for my parents until some farmer decided he was a stray and a nuisance.

And now we have arrived at a few truisms about the relationship between dogs and humans. First, dogs are more loyal and observant than humans. They don't always understand our wishes or intentions, but they work like hell to know them. Second, dogs are often the first casualty as they puzzle through and react to the arbitrary decisions we make. And third, my mother has a way of telling a story that will slay you—I mean, like plunge a knife right into tender flesh and twist it for good measure.

I spend a fair amount of time online watching videos of humans trying to save wild animals in peril—bears wandering around with buckets stuck on their snouts, sea turtles tangled in discarded fishing nets, a hawk with a wing tangled in barbed wire, a flailing diddle of beached dolphins, a fox with its head stuck through a wheel well. In these videos, humans try to undo the damage done by our own creations. I watch with a mixture of joy, watching people risk the jaws of wild things to put a hand in and intervene, and shame, at what our human necessities and luxuries have wrought upon the wild.

Similarly, I never fail to get caught up in domestic dramas as people constantly lose and recover their pets on Facebook: "Baxter spotted crossing Grand Avenue," someone will write, or joyfully announce, "Piper has been found!"

About a month after Musa went on the run, perhaps one of the strangest lost pet cases was posted on Ames People. A family was loading some livestock onto a trailer and two calves made a break for it inside the city limits. The Herefords were on the town for almost forty-eight hours.

The owners appealed to the public. "Just saw one calf by the Oakwood apartments," someone helpfully responded. The Ames Police Department got into the act, posting a missing bovine report on their Facebook page. After both calves were finally captured, people celebrated. "That was really a mooving story," one person wrote.

That last afternoon that we tried to catch Musa, when his owner came over to the cul-de-sac and walked the creek calling the dog's name, who knows if Musa was within earshot? It was getting dark and rainy, and the autumn bite was in the air. I could see that Musa's owner was jet-lagged, and to be honest, I didn't feel like slogging around in the storm either. We agreed to try again first thing in the morning.

I promised to put out some food. "He'll probably weigh 400 pounds by the time you catch him," I joked. "Yeah," he replied, "he's not gonna fit in his house." But as it got darker and colder that night and the rain really started to pelt, I regretted our decision. I texted, "Poor little buddy out in the rain."

Early the next morning, I got a text from Musa's owner. Animal control had just called to let him know that Musa had been hit by a car on South Dakota Avenue and was dead. From the state of the body, they estimated it had happened around six that morning. It was dark and wet outside. The dog was black and low to the ground. That road is busy, and traffic moves fast. The driver probably didn't even realize they had hit something.

Whenever people lose a pet, someone always says that they've gone over the rainbow bridge. I don't imagine there's anything so euphemistic about an animal dying. Other people will offer, "circle of life," an explanation that always feels cavalier. It's easy to say circle of life when you're not the one around whom death has drawn a circle.

After I adopted Buttons and Benjamin at five months old, I was required to take them to a vet within a few days to have their health checked. My friend who has Newfoundland dogs recommended Liz McClure who runs a veterinary hospital in Boone, Iowa.

As Dr. McClure gently examined and handled the puppies, who were skittish and feral in those first weeks, I appreciated her patience and the way she answered my bonehead questions. She declared both pups healthy and sound.

"I feel like I won the lottery," I exclaimed.

"Ah," she said, "I bet they think they won the lottery." I hope that she was right.

I was such an inexperienced dog owner that I didn't know the most basic things. The first time I put them on leashes and took them for a walk, for example, we got outside and just ran and ran and ran through the open fields. They looked up at me incredulous, wide smiles and wild tongues. This took some un-doing when it came time to establish a regular walking routine. Now they know so much. I have to spell so many words: cookie, outside, treat, greenie, walk, car.

Buttons and Benjamin are ten now. Bichons have a life ex-pectancy of around thirteen to fourteen years, so every morning when we wake up and I see their eager faces, ready to go out in the yard and discover what the rabbits have done overnight, I try to look at them with the understanding that our time together is short.

The morning that Musa died, I wondered why he would venture across South Dakota. He'd seemed to stay on the north-east side of that busy intersection for the two weeks while he was on the run. Maybe he was venturing for the pond south of Kum & Go where migrating ducks and geese were congregat-ing. Or maybe he was sensing the big world further afield across

Highway 30, beyond which there were acres of Iowa cornfields and endless woods and creeks and tangled meadows. So much hunting ground.

Over that last week of Musa's free-ranging, I had detected a diminishing acknowledgment of my voice. The first few days, he had been tempted, almost stepping toward me when I called. But by the end, as soon as he heard anything related to humans, even the creak of a door, he'd turn tail and run. He was an unneutered male Dachshund, bred to go to ground and hunt burrowing things. Perhaps he was happy coming into his truest nature.

I'm going to think of Musa as I remember our last Tippy—willful and sentient as the rest of us, following their noses, problem-solving their survival into an uncertain future. We can only try to keep up with them when they want to run. It hurts when their lives branch away and we must travel on alone. Because to love a dog is to prepare to someday have your heart broken.

Carte Blanche

As we were packing up the Chevy with the things I planned to take to college, my father handed me a checkbook from the Stock Growers Bank. It looked odd and official in his hands—legal, even—and nothing like the buckets of milk or the hay bales or any of the other things of agriculture that I usually saw him carrying around. Inside the plastic navy blue cover, tucked into the crease, was a stack of bound checks with my name on them.

"Use these," he said, "to buy what you need while you're away."

Over the years, sometimes at the end of harvest or when the livestock was loaded up and taken off for sale, my father would make vague references to the money he was setting aside for us kids—let's say, equal to the price of one calf for each of us—in payment for helping him and Mother with the milking and the work in the fields that year.

I don't think any of us ever pinned him down about the details. Somehow, in our family (and I'm not sure how this was accomplished, because I don't recall ever being yelled at about it) we just understood that to talk about money was low and rude. Also, to ask too many questions was low and rude. So it only followed that to ask too many questions about money was not only low and rude but also impertinent.

But here was the checkbook in my hands now, evidence that the socking away of calf money had occurred.

Prior to this, I'd lived a cash-only life. I didn't need much. I had a little job waitressing at Maggie's Café in high school to buy the luxuries. Then, as now, I spent most of whatever I made on three things—books, clothes, and music. Even at that moment when I held my first checkbook in my hands, I had no idea how it worked.

But once at college, I took to writing checks like a natural, like a real pro. I learned that there were more things in the world to want than I'd previously imagined: shoes in black, brown, and tan; sandals in low and high heels; dresses, sweaters, and skirts; raincoats, umbrellas, and hats. Makeup and jewelry. Books on philosophy and history. Albums for bands that weren't even on the radio.

With my new college friends, other girls from small towns around North Dakota set loose now in the big city, I also discovered eating out. In Napoleon, my hometown, there was pretty much only Maggie's Café and the pool hall downtown, where you could still get the best order of French fries ever made for twenty-five cents. But in Bismarck, there were places like A & B Pizza and the Big Boy Drive-In. I don't think we ever splurged on expensive restaurants, but we skipped out on the college food service enough to eat our way across town. We all gained the requisite Freshman 10 Pounds.

My monthly bank statements must have read like an ethnographic study of the odd habits and proclivities of this new creature my parents were discovering me to be, a female college freshman. It would have been better than satellite tracking or inserting a computer chip under my skin, because once I went paper, I went paper. I don't think I ever learned how to get cash out of my checking account.

I mention the bank statement now only to point out two other amazing facts that I didn't know at the time about checking accounts—that a bank statement was mailed out each month, and that it was being sent to my parents who, I presume, studied it carefully.

About eight months into this experiment, my dad called me up and said, "Well, we're closing down the checking account."

"Why?" I asked, incredulous. It seemed to be working so marvelously.

That's when I learned about the bank statements that were coming to my parents along with the monthly pack of cancelled checks, those little numbered slips of paper that I had wildly signed, torn out along the perforations, and strewn across the counters of stores and restaurants in Bismarck.

"But I still have plenty of checks," I told my father. And that's when I learned another stunning thing—that money had to be put into the account to counterbalance the writing of the checks. I don't recall anyone ever mentioning the part about making deposits, or maybe he told me about checks and balances, but it simply fell from my head like algebra and chemistry and calculus had.

Even before I understood all the intricacies of banking—even after—I marveled at the counter checks in the café and stores in my hometown. In the Red Owl and the Rexall Drug near the chewing gum and the cigarette lighters, in Maggie's Café near the mints and the toothpicks in their cellophane wrappers, a tattered pack of counter checks from the Stock Growers Bank was always tucked in the crevice between the napkin holder and the cash register.

The counter checks were left blank of any information—convenience checks for people who may have forgotten their checkbooks at home. Not only the normal places on the check for the "date," the "dollar," and the "pay to the order of" were left blank. Not only the long line for the signature was left blank, and the spot marked "memo," where you could write "rent" or "fishing gear" to remind yourself what you'd just spent money on. But also the upper left corner of the check where the account holder's name and address usually was printed and the long bottom edge of the check where the account number was shown were all left blank. It seemed like *carte blanche*, courtesy of the Stock Growers Bank.

It appears naïve and quaint on the surface, but I soon understood that what keeps counter checks from being an embezzler's dream is the safety net of the small town, the merchant's knowledge of all of his customers, the families they belong to, and what their history has been. A small town is a claustrophobically finite world. Everybody's watching; everybody knows. And a small town is not a place where you want to start bouncing checks, counter or otherwise. It's like fouling your own nest, or, as my father used to say, "shitting too close to the house."

About my own derelict checking account—later, I discovered that the banker, Parkas, would call my father when my checking account ran low. "Debbie is overdrawn again," he'd say. Then my dad would run downtown and deposit a few hundred more dollars. Years later my mother told me that they would sift through the checks I had written—$1.25 at Dairy Queen, $2.33 at Village Inn—and shake their heads. They were paying five dollars for every overdraft.

I'm sure they were devastated by the waste of it, and I'm certain my father found it hard to fathom why I needed so much in the world in excess of the price of one calf sold to slaughter each year.

Everything I think and write about home these days makes me feel like crying, because so much of it is gone, pushed out of the way through the natural forces of time, erased through death.

When I remember the solemn gesture of my father handing me my first checkbook as I leave home for college, never to re-turn—although none of us knows that yet—when I think about him rushing down to the Stock Growers Bank to deposit two hundred more dollars to cover my checks for lipstick or panty hose, I have to get up and walk around a while. I have to unload the dishwasher or play with the dogs.

Because my father has been gone from the world for almost twenty years now, and I doubt I will ever find anyone who loves me as much as he did. And that world of home, that world of checks and balances that he believed in has changed so much, beyond anything he would have imagined.

When I drive through western North Dakota these days, I think of him. When I see the flare pits burning off natural gas around the oil wells, burning off natural resources into the al-ready fragile atmosphere just because no one wants to slow down long enough to collect it, I think of him.

When I see the oil and water tankers navigating slippery country roads and read about the catastrophic accidents that re-sult on the highways; when I hear of pipeline ruptures emptying thousands of barrels of crude into a farmer's field; of trainloads of fuel exploding near a small North Dakota town; of fracking flu-id and oil and saline water spills occurring almost daily in rural regions where people are dependent on well water, I think about how much this is all going to cost.

Because it's a finite world. Everybody's watching; everybody knows. And I wonder who is going to step forward to pay for this, to settle the bill when it comes due. And I think I have an idea about who that might be.

The world my father trained me to live in is not the world I live in now. So I must shed some of his training. To talk about money, about checks and balances, and who's going to pay for all this is not low or rude. To ask a second question, or a third question, or even a fourth or fifth is not impertinent. Because we have so many questions that need asking.

That day, after my father called me at college to tell me he was closing down my checking account, he said he would wait a few weeks until the checks had all cleared. After that, for the next few days, I went on a spending frenzy. I bought toothpaste and toilet paper; rugs and comforters and bed sheets; pajamas and bathrobes; nail polish, shampoo, and face moisturizer. I bought chocolate bars and camera film and underwear. It felt like the end. I tried to buy everything that I thought I was going to need for the rest of my life. But it wasn't the end. It was just the end of *carte blanche*, the beginning of resource management, of life stewardship, of understanding limits, of maturity.

And I'm not going to beat myself up about not understanding how money worked. Just recently, a friend of mine told me about how her teenage daughter had asked her for money, and when my friend said, "No, honey, I don't have any money," her daughter said, "Yes you do, Mom. All you have to do is put your card in the machine and it will give you money."

So maybe it's just something developmental that we all must go through, like that period before frontal lobe development when we feel as if nothing can touch or hurt us, and we think the whole world is just a space left blank for us to write our wishes upon.

And it would never even occur to us that someone is running around in the background cleaning up our messes, that someone we love fiercely is paying the highest prices just to make good on the things to which we have so foolishly committed our signatures.

Acknowledgments

The author is grateful to the editors in the following journals in which the following essays originally appeared, sometimes in different forms:

"The Art of the Cheer," *Fast Break to Line Break: Poets on the Art of Basketball*

"At 79, My Mother Decides to Plant Trees," *Fourth Genre: Explorations in Nonficton*

"Carte Blanche," *On Second Thought: The Sense of Place Issue*

"The Death of a Lost Dog," *The Iowan*

"Ephemera," *Cream City Review*

"The Night We Landed on the Moon" (under the title "The Moon"), *North Dakota Quarterly*

"Living to Tell the Tale," *The Fourth River*

"Losing the Meadow," *Alligator Juniper*

"Mrs. Schumacher Busts a Nut," *Cimarron Review*

"Not All There," *Prairie Gold: An Anthology of the American Heartland*

"Odessa!" (under the title, "The Political Migrations of Wheat"), *New Letters*

"Refusing Nostalgia," *On Second Thought: The Journey Stories Issue*

"Perils of Travel," *Gulf Coast*

"The Taste of Home," *On Second Thought: The Sense of Place Issue*

"Thirteen Ways of Looking at the Weather," *Prairie Weather: Harvest Book Series*

"Those Desirable Things," *Event Magazine*

I'm grateful to the National Endowment for the Arts for an NEA Fellowship and the College of Liberal Arts & Sciences at Iowa State University for an LAS Faculty Fellowship that supported the completion of this research.

I also wish to thank Humanities North Dakota for three invited traveling residencies (2013, 2015, 2017) that enabled me to travel back to North Dakota and teach creative writing workshops all around the state.

Thanks to the Arcus Center for Social Justice Leadership at Kalamazoo College for a Social Justice Fellowship in the Spring of 2015 that allowed me to complete this research.

I am especially grateful to my editor at NDSU Press, Suzzanne Kelley, who saw something worthwhile in this manuscript and expertly guided it to this finished form.

Finally, special thanks to Dr. Roger Hanson, an alumnus of Iowa State University, who established the Roger S. Hanson Faculty Support Fund in Creative Writing, which enabled me to complete some of the work contained here. As the inaugural recipient of this gift, I am forever grateful to Dr. Hanson for his support of my work.

Works Cited

Boym, Svetlana. (2001). *The Future of Nostalgia.* Basic Books.

Cather, Willa. (1996). *O Pioneers!* Book-of-the-Month-Club.

Eliade, Mircea. (1954). *The Myth of the Eternal Return: Or, Cosmos and History.* Princeton University Press.

Kimmelman, Michael. (23 June 2009). "Elgin Marble Argument in a New Light," *The New York Times.*

McDonough, William. (2003). "Address to the Woods Hole Symposium." https://mcdonough.com/writings/address-woods-hole-symposium/.

Momaday, N. Scott. (1997). *The Man Made of Words: Essays, Stories, Passages.* St. Martin's Press.

Scarry, Elaine. (1999). *On Beauty and Being Just.* Princeton University Press.

Thomas, Helen. (2008). "Colonizing the Land: *Heimat* and the Constructed Landscapes of Mexico's Ciudad Universitaria. Felipe Hernandez, editor. *Transculturation. Cities, Spaces and Architectures in Latin America.* Brill.

Wohlleben, Peter. (2015). *The Hidden Life of Trees: What They Feel, How They Communicate—Discoveries from a Secret World.* Greystone.

Woolf, Virginia. (1975). *A Room of One's Own.* Harvest/HBJ.

WPA Interview Archives. (1939). North Dakota State Historical Library.

WPA Interview Archives. (1939). Borr, Peter. "Accidental and Sudden Deaths," Supplementary Report. Emmons County. North Dakota State Historical Library.

About the Author

Debra Marquart is the author of six books including *Small Buried Things: Poems* (2015), *The Horizontal World: Growing Up Wild in the Middle of Nowhere* (2007), and a co-edited anthology of experimental writing, *Nothing to Declare: A Guide to the Prose Sequence* (2016). Marquart is a recipient of an NEA Fellowship, a PEN USA Nonfiction Award, the Wachtmeister Award for Excellence in the Arts, the Normal Poetry Prize, the Paumanok Poetry Award, and *Elle Magazine*'s Elle Lettres Award, among others. A singer/songwriter, Marquart is a member of The Bone People, a jazz-poetry rhythm & blues project with whom she has recorded two CDs: *Orange Parade* (original songs) and *A Regular Dervish* (jazz-poetry). A Distinguished Professor of Liberal Arts & Sciences in the MFA Program in Creative Writing and Environment at Iowa State University, Marquart is also the Senior Editor of *Flyway: Journal of Writing & Environment*, and she teaches in the Stonecoast Low-Residency MFA Program at the University of Southern Maine. In 2019, Marquart was appointed the Poet Laureate of the State of Iowa.

About the Press

North Dakota State University Press (NDSU Press) exists to stimulate and coordinate interdisciplinary regional scholarship. These regions include the Red River Valley, the state of North Dakota, the plains of North America (comprising both the Great Plains of the United States and the prairies of Canada), and comparable regions of other continents. We publish peer reviewed regional scholarship shaped by national and international events and comparative studies.

Neither topic nor discipline limits the scope of NDSU Press publications. We consider manuscripts in any field of learning. We define our scope, however, by a regional focus in accord with the press's mission. Generally, works published by NDSU Press address regional life directly, as the subject of study. Such works contribute to scholarly knowledge of region (that is, discovery of new knowledge) or to public consciousness of region (that is, dissemination of information, or interpretation of regional experience). Where regions abroad are treated, either for comparison or because of ties to those North American regions of primary concern to the press, the linkages are made plain. For nearly three-quarters of a century, NDSU Press has published substantial trade books, but the line of publications is not limited to that genre. We also publish textbooks (at any level), reference books, anthologies, reprints, papers, proceedings, and monographs. The press also considers works of poetry or fiction, provided they are established regional classics or they promise to assume landmark or reference status for the region. We select biographical or autobiographical works carefully for their prospective contribution to regional knowledge and culture. All publications, in whatever genre, are of such quality and substance as to embellish the imprint of NDSU Press.

We changed our imprint to North Dakota State University Press in January 2016. Prior to that, and since 1950, we published as the North Dakota Institute for Regional Studies Press. We continue to operate under the umbrella of the North Dakota Institute for Regional Studies, located at North Dakota State University.